New Directions for
Child and Adolescent
Development

William Damon
EDITOR-IN-CHIEF

Connections Between Theory of Mind and Sociomoral Development

Jodie A. Baird
Bryan W. Sokol
EDITORS

Number 103 • Spring 2004
Jossey-Bass
San Francisco

CONNECTIONS BETWEEN THEORY OF MIND AND SOCIOMORAL DEVELOPMENT
Jodie A. Baird, Bryan W. Sokol (eds.)
New Directions for Child and Adolescent Development, no. 103
William Damon, Editor-in-Chief

© 2004 Wiley Periodicals, Inc., a Wiley company. All rights reserved.

No part of this publication may be reproduced, stored in a retrieval system, or transmitted in any form or by any means, electronic, mechanical, photocopying, recording, scanning, or otherwise, except as permitted under Sections 107 or 108 of the 1976 United States Copyright Act, without either the prior written permission of the Publisher or authorization through payment of the appropriate per-copy fee to the Copyright Clearance Center, 222 Rosewood Drive, Danvers, MA 01923, (978) 750-8400, fax (978) 646-8600. Requests to the Publisher for permission should be addressed to the Permissions Department, John Wiley & Sons, Inc., 111 River Street, Hoboken, NJ 07030, (201) 748-6011, fax (201) 748-6008, www.wiley.com/go/permissions.

Microfilm copies of issues and articles are available in 16mm and 35mm, as well as microfiche in 105mm, through University Microfilms Inc., 300 North Zeeb Road, Ann Arbor, Michigan 48106-1346.

ISSN 1520-3247   electronic ISSN 1534-8687

NEW DIRECTIONS FOR CHILD AND ADOLESCENT DEVELOPMENT is part of The Jossey-Bass Education Series and is published quarterly by Wiley Subscription Services, Inc., a Wiley company, at Jossey-Bass, 989 Market Street, San Francisco, California 94103-1741. Periodicals postage paid at San Francisco, California, and at additional mailing offices. Postmaster: Send address changes to New Directions for Child and Adolescent Development, Jossey-Bass, 989 Market Street, San Francisco, CA 94103-1741.

New Directions for Child and Adolescent Development is indexed in Biosciences Information Service, Current Index to Journals in Education (ERIC), Psychological Abstracts, and Sociological Abstracts.

SUBSCRIPTIONS cost $90.00 for individuals and $195.00 for institutions, agencies, and libraries.

EDITORIAL CORRESPONDENCE should be sent to the Editor-in-Chief, William Damon, Stanford Center on Adolescence, Cypress Building C, Stanford University, Stanford, CA 94305.

Jossey-Bass Web address: www.josseybass.com

Contents

EDITORS' NOTES　　1
Jodie A. Baird, Bryan W. Sokol

1. "Is" and "Ought": Moral Judgments About the World as Understood　　3
Cecilia Wainryb
The author considers a framework for understanding how beliefs about the way the world is bear on moral decisions. This interplay of moral concepts and factual beliefs figures prominently in the explanation of moral diversity and in the explanation of children's understanding and tolerance of moral diversity.

2. From Mechanical to Autonomous Agency: The Relationship Between Children's Moral Judgments and Their Developing Theories of Mind　　19
Bryan W. Sokol, Michael J. Chandler, Christopher Jones
If the current gap between theories-of-mind research and the field of sociomoral development is to be successfully bridged, then greater attention must be given over to addressing how both "professional" and "folk" psychologists conceptualize human agency.

3. The Role of Mental State Understanding in the Development of Moral Cognition and Moral Action　　37
Jodie A. Baird, Janet Wilde Astington
The authors address developmental changes in children's motives-based moral reasoning. Drawing on research with typically developing and behavior-disordered children, they report relations among moral cognition, mental state understanding, and real-world social behavior.

4. Altruism, Prudence, and Theory of Mind in Preschoolers　　51
Chris Moore, Shannon Macgillivray
The authors argue that theory of mind is not sufficient to make children act prosocially. Individual differences in the tendency to value the concerns of others likely play an important role. The distinction between the cognitive and motivational aspects of behavioral control is illustrated in a longitudinal study.

5. Bridging the Gap Between Theory of Mind and Moral Reasoning 63
Reasoning
Janet Wilde Astington
The gap between theory of mind and moral reasoning research is more apparent than real due to the different emphases in the two fields. However, a more fundamental gap, which is the one between reasoning abilities and behavior, exists in both fields, and this requires investigation.

6. Mind and Morality 73
Peter H. Kahn Jr.
This chapter examines why the fields of theory of mind and moral development have remained largely divided over the years and how they can now enrich one another.

Index 85

Editors' Notes

> When moral worth is in question, it is not a matter of actions which one sees but of their inner principles which one does not see.
>
> —Immanuel Kant

The notion that our mental and moral lives are related in intimate ways hardly seems to constitute a new idea. Not only is the connection between our mental states and our moral decisions and behavior made throughout our own daily lives as folk psychologists, a topic taken up by many of the authors here, it also has deep intellectual roots, as evidenced by Kant's famous remark quoted above. Even in our own academic discipline, this theme of mind and morals resonates throughout the classic works of Piaget (1965), Heider (1958), and Kohlberg (1981, 1984), to name just a few.

How, then, has such a familiar theme managed to make its way into a series dedicated to promoting new ideas and directions in the field? Are the research efforts represented here so groundbreaking that they redefine the fundamental connection between mental and moral life? The honest and simple answer is no. But, then again, our ambitions for this volume, and the 2001 Society for Research in Child Development symposium out of which it grew, have never been to *redefine* this relationship. Rather, each of the contributions here in some way seeks to *refine* much of what we already know, or at least suspect, about the complex interaction between children's conceptions of the mind and their sociomoral development. These more modest goals have not tapered our own enthusiasm for this work, and they should not deter potential readers from pushing forward. This is because our real ambition has less to do with profiling new research paradigms and presenting novel data (although we hope to achieve that too) than it has with opening a dialogue between two research traditions that are at increasing risk of becoming cut off from one another. As such, the contributors to this volume are researchers whose work can be seen to straddle the divide between the theory-of-mind and moral development research enterprises. Together, we have worked to address two central questions. First, how do children's conceptions of the mind affect their moral judgments? Second, does children's mental state understanding influence the moral quality of their own behavior?

The volume speaks to each of these questions in turn. In particular, the first two chapters examine the link between theory of mind and moral reasoning. In Chapter One, Cecilia Wainryb explores how children's epistemological understanding influences their moral evaluations, with an emphasis on the differential impact of factual beliefs versus moral beliefs. Bryan Sokol, Michael Chandler, and Christopher Jones investigate in Chapter Two whether and how children's emerging conception of human agency relates to the sophistication of their moral judgments. The subsequent two chapters concentrate on relations between children's reasoning about the mind and the ethics of their own behavior. More specifically, in Chapter Three, Jodie Baird and Janet Astington examine how children's ability to use mental state information in evaluating others' behavior relates to their own social conduct, particularly aggression. In Chapter Four, Chris Moore and Shannon Macgillivray address the link between children's theory of mind and their tendency toward future-oriented prudence and prosocial behavior.

The volume concludes with separate commentaries from Janet Astington and Peter Kahn Jr. As scholars with respective interests in the theory-of-mind and moral development literatures, they assure us that these two research traditions have much to share with each other. We hope that this volume provides a beginning.

Jodie A. Baird
Bryan W. Sokol
Editors

References

Heider, F. *The Psychology of Interpersonal Relations.* New York: Wiley, 1958.
Kant, I. *Foundations of the Metaphysics of Morals* (L. W. Beck, trans.). New York: Macmillan, 1959. (Originally published 1785.)
Kohlberg, L. *The Philosophy of Moral Development: Moral Stages and the Idea of Justice.* San Francisco: HarperSanFrancisco, 1981.
Kohlberg, L. *The Psychology of Moral Development: The Nature and Validity of Moral Stages.* San Francisco: HarperSanFrancisco, 1984.
Piaget, J. *The Moral Judgment of the Child* (M. Gabain, trans.). New York: Free Press, 1965. (Originally published 1932.)

JODIE A. BAIRD is a postdoctoral fellow in the Department of Human Development and Applied Psychology at the Ontario Institute for Studies in Education of the University of Toronto.

BRYAN W. SOKOL is assistant professor of psychology at Simon Fraser University, Burnaby, British Columbia.

> While abiding by the injunction against deriving "ought" statements from "is" statements, the author considers ways in which the "is" bears on the "ought." Persons, it is proposed, make moral judgments and decisions about the world as they understand it to be.

"Is" and "Ought": Moral Judgments About the World as Understood

Cecilia Wainryb

> When Julia was about four years old, she enjoyed pretending to be a dog and used to sniff and lick everything around her. A friend, aghast at the sight of Julia licking the floor, patiently explained to her the concept of germs: "There are teeny tiny bugs that we can't see at all, but they are everywhere, on the floor, on the furniture, on everything, and if they get in your mouth and your body, they'll make you sick." Without hesitating, Julia rebutted: "MOOOOOM, she's telling a lie!"

Do matters of fact—beliefs, understandings, and theories about the way the world is—have any significant bearing on moral decisions? Starting with Hume (1978), philosophers within the English-language tradition have written extensively about the validity of the fact-value distinction and the is-to-ought fallacy. In spite of direct and indirect challenges by a number of contemporary thinkers (Anscombe, 1981; MacIntyre, 1984; Putnam, 1987), the distinction between matters of fact and matters of morality and the injunction against deriving "ought" statements from "is" statements remain at the heart of nonrelativistic approaches to morality (Dworkin, 1985; Frankena, 1973; Hare, 1952; Rawls, 1971).

Within the discipline of psychology, it was Lawrence Kohlberg who first and cogently argued about the fundamental importance of these meta-ethical considerations for the study of moral development. In spite of the bit of teasing veiled in the title of his classical piece *From Is to Ought: How to Commit the Naturalistic Fallacy and Get Away with It* (1971), Kohlberg's central message was an unequivocal admonition against both conflating matters of fact and value and using the facts of cultural variability in moral standards to advance or justify the notion of ethical relativism. (The title refers to the very mild form of the naturalistic fallacy and that which Kohlberg urged his readers to engage in: that the findings of psychological research on moral development, that is, "is," have relevance for and can be used to inform normative ethics, that is, "ought.") In his developmental model, Kohlberg posited that the differentiation of "is" and "ought," which he viewed as a fundamental feature of mature moral concepts, does not exist from the outset but rather is constructed gradually throughout development. Thinking at the lower stages involves a confusion of "is" and "ought"; judgments are made in reference to personal and conventional concerns and are contingent on aspects of reality such as existing laws, norms, or expectations. As moral development progresses, matters of "ought" are increasingly extricated from the "is"; moral concepts become prescriptive, and thinking becomes equilibrated.

In contrast to Kohlberg's unqualified view that moral judgments at the highest stages are no longer derived from or contingent on the "is," his thinking in regard to the role of matters of fact once moral concepts have become prescriptive was not conclusive. For example, Kohlberg explicitly recognized that moral judgments are "the product of an interaction between moral assumptions and assumptions of fact" (Kohlberg and Elfenbein, 1976, p. 252) and identified that interaction between moral and factual elements as responsible for the conflicting moral judgments (that is, contents) that may be observed within a stage. Whereas those statements suggest that Kohlberg may have regarded the role of factual assumptions as stable across development, he also made a number of statements that appear to contradict this conclusion. For example, in discussing the development of reasoning about the death penalty, Kohlberg stated that "the higher the stage, the greater the likelihood that individuals at that stage will agree not only in the structure of their reasoning but in the content of their judgments as well" (p. 276). In a postscript to a later (1981) revision of that article, Kohlberg added that the attainment of stage 6 generates uniform moral condemnation of the death penalty because stage 6 judgments rest on moral principles "that are entirely independent of factual assumptions" (p. 293).

Ultimately, Kohlberg's position in this regard is ambiguous because he did not attend to these issues in any systematic fashion. Whereas he investigated in detail the forms that judgments took at various stages of development and noted the contingencies of early judgments on nonmoral matters, such as expectations and rules, he did not examine the role that factual assumptions play once moral concepts become differentiated from the "is" and attain prescriptivity. Indeed, until quite recently (Turiel, Hildebrandt, and Wainryb, 1991; Wainryb, 1991, 1993), no research was conducted examining the relation of morality and beliefs about matters of fact. But one may quite reasonably ask whether perhaps there is no reason to attend to factual considerations in relation to prescriptive moral concepts if the very idea of prescriptivity implies that moral concepts are not derived from or contingent on factual considerations.

In this chapter, I consider a framework for attending to the relation between matters of fact and morality that is grounded on the domain-specific model of development (Turiel, 1983, 1998). The gist of my proposition is that prescriptive moral concepts are applied against a background of factual beliefs and understandings; therefore, beliefs about matters of fact have a bearing on moral thinking throughout development. I discuss how prescriptive moral concepts and factual beliefs come together in children's moral judgments and then consider children's understandings of how moral concepts and factual beliefs come together in moral judgments.

The Interplay of Moral and Factual Beliefs in Children's Judgments

Whereas Kohlberg's global stage model posits that morality (the "ought") starts out as indistinguishable from convention and custom (the "is"), Turiel's domain-specific model posits that thought is organized according to distinct epistemological categories. In support of the domain-specific model, evidence from several dozen studies has demonstrated that by the age of three or four, children already possess moral concepts—ways of thinking about welfare and justice—that are not contingent on nonmoral considerations but are prescriptive and generalizable. Insofar as children understand an event as implicating an agent who intentionally mistreats or inflicts harm on an unwilling victim, they bring to bear their moral concepts and judge the agent's behavior to be morally wrong (for comprehensive reviews of this research, see Smetana, 1995; Turiel, 1998). But how do children (and, more generally, persons) come to understand that an event involves mistreatment or intentional harm? People cannot merely procure an unmediated record of the facts of events; this is not how people know moral events (or anything else).

Long before the notions of subjective construal and interpretation entered the scholarly discourse by way of postmodernist writings, Gestalt psychologists had demonstrated that "objects of judgment" (whatever individuals make judgments about) are not fixed and do not merely reside in or coincide with the facts of events. Objects of judgment, they argued, are cognitively created and transformed (Asch, 1952). When individuals bring to bear their moral concepts on a particular event, they do so with regard to the event not as it "really is" but as they construe (understand, believe) it to be. Consider, as an example, four-year-old Julia from the beginning of this chapter. When Julia judged that her friend was lying (and implicitly demanded that the liar get in trouble), she was proceeding on the basis of her understanding of the facts of the event ("Of course there are no bugs that *no one* can see," she added later). Whereas these issues were not considered by researchers of moral development, Asch (1952) astutely noted the fundamental role of factual beliefs and understandings in moral decisions (see also Duncker, 1939; Wertheimer, 1935). Guided by Asch's early insights, we incorporated into our domain-specific investigations of moral development systematic analyses of the ways in which beliefs and understandings about matters of fact bear on the application of moral concepts.

In a series of studies (Shaw and Wainryb, 1999; Turiel, Hildebrandt, and Wainryb, 1991; Wainryb, 1991, 1993; Wainryb and Ford, 1998; Wainryb and Laupa, 1994; Wainryb, Shaw, and Maianau, 1998) with participants between their preschool and college years, we demonstrated that moral judgments are made in reference to specific beliefs about the relevant facts and, furthermore, that differences in moral judgments are systematically associated with those beliefs. For example, when asked about corporal punishment, children and adolescents (ages eleven through twenty-one) spontaneously discussed their beliefs and understandings concerning whether learning and remembering are in fact aided by the experience of pain (Wainryb, 1991). Their beliefs in this regard were not uniform (some believed that feeling pain helps children learn and remember; others believed that it does not), and their judgments of corporal punishment were systematically associated with those factual beliefs (those who believed that pain promotes learning judged corporal punishment positively; those who believed that pain does not promote learning judged it negatively). Similar patterns of results were obtained for young children's reasoning about unequal treatment and unequal distribution of resources in the classroom (Wainryb and Ford, 1998), for school-aged children's and adolescents' reasoning about situations in which younger and older persons were treated differently (Wainryb, 1991), and for adolescents' and young adults' reasoning about abortion, pornography (Turiel, Hildebrandt, and Wainryb, 1991), and capital punishment (Wainryb and Laupa, 1994). In each case, the evidence indicated that children make moral judgments in reference to their specific factual beliefs and that conflicting moral judgments are systematically associated with those beliefs. In each case, the evidence also indicated that participants who made conflicting moral judgments nevertheless endorsed identical moral concepts; for example, regardless of how participants judged corporal punishment, all stated that it is morally wrong to inflict harm on others intentionally. As a whole, this body of findings furnished systematic support for our proposition that throughout development, prescriptive moral concepts are applied against a background of factual understandings and beliefs about relevant aspects of reality and, furthermore, demonstrated that diversity in moral judgments can be examined in reference to diversity in factual beliefs and understandings.

The bearing of factual beliefs on moral thinking has far-reaching implications. Through the lens of different factual understandings and beliefs about reality, instances of seemingly unmitigated physical harm can emerge as morally acceptable and instances of seemingly benign behaviors as morally wrong. Take as an example the practice of putting one's elderly parents to death. This practice is presumed to be common in cultures where it is believed, as a matter of fact, that people continue to exist in the afterlife with the same condition of health they had at the time of death (Asch, 1952). Through the lens of this particular understanding of the facts of the afterlife, a practice that seems eminently harmful to us is understood to be the means for ensuring the eternal welfare of one's parents and judged to be a moral obligation toward one's parents. Although this example is unusual in that it entails the taking of life, the phenomenon it illustrates is by no means rare. It is not uncommon, even today, for seemingly noxious practices, such as bloodletting and female circumcision, and seemingly innocuous personal or conventional preferences, such as eating certain foods or wearing certain clothes, to carry the opposite moral status in societies where they are seen through the lens of different factual beliefs (Turiel, Killen, and Helwig, 1987; Wainryb, 2000). As is evident in our own research, it is also not uncommon for practices to be construed and evaluated differently within societies.

It may seem as though by asserting that the meanings of "facts" are neither given in the world nor fixed but cognitively construed and transformed (to the point that an act such as putting one's parents to death becomes morally desirable), we advance the moral relativistic proposition that any one act can be morally right or morally wrong. There is, however, an important sense in which the two propositions are not equivalent. We maintain that through different construals or understandings of the facts of reality, any act can be judged as morally wrong, but only insofar as the facts are understood to signal the presence of intentional harm. This is not akin to saying, as moral relativists do, that the relation between act and moral judgment is arbitrary. It only seems as though by acknowledging that persons make moral judgments in reference to their construals of the world we have opened the door to moral relativism and subjectivity. I suggest that by recognizing the psychological reality of how people know the facts of the world, we actually lay out the basis for detecting the prescriptive and generalizable nature of moral thinking.

Although this may be plain and apparent, it bears making it explicit that the process by which people come to "know" the facts of the world introduces a fair amount of diversity and subjectivity into moral thinking. For myriad reasons, individuals arrive, at least some of the time, at different factual understandings and beliefs regarding one or another aspect of reality. It is therefore possible, and indeed quite likely, for moral judgments to be made in reference to factual beliefs that are inaccurate. Is that good or bad? Inasmuch as ours is a proposition about the psychology of moral thinking, it just is. Moreover, although children's understandings of the world are likely to be mistaken or constrained in systematic ways, hardly anyone would maintain that adults' understandings of the world are uniformly accurate. Therefore, our proposition is that "it just is, throughout development." Throughout development, persons apply prescriptive moral concepts to reality as they understand it to be, and sometimes the understandings from which they proceed are mistaken.

But what if factual beliefs and understandings are not merely mistaken? Some might find fault with our proposition not because of the concern that the factual beliefs underlying moral judgments may turn out to be inaccurate but because factual beliefs are not truly factual. People, the argument goes, unconsciously bring themselves to believe whatever enables them to rationalize their self-serving choices (Bandura, 1991). From this perspective, factual beliefs are moral (that is, immoral) choices in disguise.

Although solid experimental evidence in this regard is scarce, in principle I do not see the phenomenon of rationalization as being inconsistent with a constructivist view of development and cognition (Wainryb, 2000). In the course of the constructivist process, previous understandings inevitably guide new understandings; it is therefore conceivable that previous moral choices might guide attempts at understanding and interpreting new facts and that the ensuing factual understandings would be informed by moral considerations. Because it is also not unusual for simultaneously held conflicting beliefs to remain unintegrated, it is possible that an individual's experience in this regard might not be fully deliberate or conscious. Altogether, therefore, it makes sense to acknowledge the possibility that some factual beliefs might not be fully independent from previous moral choices and might function, in a nondeliberate way, as means for evading inner conflict. (I am thankful to Bryan Sokol for pointing out that because of their striving for coherence within a system of beliefs, self-serving beliefs might also, and perhaps more adequately, be characterized as self-preserving. See also Nucci and Lee, 1993.)

Acknowledging this possibility is not the same as saying that in the context of moral judgments, factual beliefs are always rationalizations. There are many ways in which children and adults who set out to understand what is true (as opposed to, deliberately or unconsciously, concealing what they believe to be true) might end up misunderstanding or misconstruing reality. Psychological research has documented multiple cognitive, social, and developmental biases that, without arising or functioning as means for rationalizing immoral decisions, systematically afflict people's understandings of reality. It is also untenable to maintain that because moral choices guide or inform some attempts at understanding factual aspects of reality, the distinction between factual and moral categories is not valid. The existence of mixtures, overlaps, and confusions between the two types of beliefs, in and of itself, does not preclude the validity of the distinction. It could be argued that the existence of hybrid cases renders the distinction not invalid but pointless, and that beliefs are better understood as located somewhere on a fact-value continuum. While that might be a viable alternative, it is unclear how the proportions of factual and value elements of beliefs can be quantified with any precision. More important, a fact-value continuum is bound to obscure the distinct developmental roots of moral and factual categories of thought (Wainryb and Turiel, 1993) and the dynamic process by which "hybrid" beliefs are constituted.

In my view, there is little to be gained by folding the distinction between factual and moral beliefs, as doing that precludes the possibility of examining how individuals coordinate moral and factual beliefs in those cases in which they can be unambiguously disentangled. Furthermore, at least in principle, the distinction between factual and moral categories has the potential for informing analyses of hybrid beliefs. Altogether, acknowledging the possibility that moral decisions might be made in reference to misconstruals of reality, only some of which are rationalizations that function as means for evading inner conflict, does not necessarily require doing away with the fact-value distinction. It does, however, point to the need for research to distinguish among types of factual misconstruals and to examine the specific ways in which children coordinate those misconstruals with their moral concepts.

Thus far, I have suggested that what appear to be morally wrong decisions are likely to be moral decisions that were made in reference to different, inaccurate, or self-serving factual beliefs. Have I then reduced all moral differences (in decisions, behaviors, practices) to factual differences? Worse still, are the "bad guys" just "misinformed"? I do concede that identifying the "misinformed" is seldom as satisfying as chasing the "bad guys," and yet our proposition does imply that at least some of the seemingly bad guys are best described as "not well informed" and some are "differently informed." Furthermore, whereas the proponents of self-serving beliefs might be "bad guys" if one thinks of those beliefs as moral choices in disguise, or "somewhat bad" (and "somewhat misinformed") if one locates those beliefs on a fact-value continuum, in our interpretation they are best understood as applying moral concepts to understandings of reality distorted by the need to maintain a sense of integrity. Unquestionably, we have shrunk considerably the universe of "bad guys." Still, our proposition that moral decisions are informed by factual understandings (and misunderstandings) of reality does not preclude, in principle, the possibility of "bad guys" who hold to immoral concepts and make immoral decisions. The admittedly vexing caveat in this regard, however, is that to assert that the difference between two decisions or behaviors is of a moral nature, it is first necessary to establish the equivalence of all underlying factual understandings. That this is a great deal easier to accomplish in the confines of the moral development lab than in real life is the source of both the strength and the constraints of our findings.

Children's Judgments About the Interplay of Moral and Factual Beliefs

Theoretical argumentation and ruminations notwithstanding, people try to identify the "bad guys" (and the morally wrong decisions) all the time. How do children go about doing that? How do they think about the variety of moral decisions and behaviors they witness? Recall once more Julia's "accusation" that her friend, who was warning Julia about germs, was lying. Most adults can recognize that when Julia judged her friend to be doing something wrong, she was proceeding from her mistaken factual belief that germs do not, as a matter of fact (how could they?), exist. How might children at different ages understand and evaluate events of this type? (Can you not conjure up in your mind the image of the ensuing "SHE is lying!" "No, SHE is lying!" tear-filled battle between the two four-year-olds?)

Our findings, as reviewed in the previous section, demonstrated that in making moral decisions, children apply prescriptive moral concepts to their varying, and sometimes mistaken, understandings of the relevant facts and, furthermore, that their varying factual understandings are consistently associated with their conflicting moral decisions. In this section, we ask whether children have a grasp of this process, whether they recognize that people who make seemingly immoral decisions may be proceeding from beliefs different from their own, and whether they are differently forgiving of people who act on the basis of the "wrong" factual beliefs and those who proceed from the "wrong" moral beliefs.

Given the broad concern with tolerance and with the developmental constraints operating on the formation of tolerant attitudes, children's understandings and evaluations of other people's decisions and practices are interesting in their own right. In the context of our examination of the ways in which beliefs about facts bear on moral thinking, our specific interest in these questions stems from two additional reasons. First, looking into children's understandings and evaluations of persons who proceed on the basis of beliefs different from their own affords us an important opportunity to ascertain whether children make distinctions in their thinking between "wrong" moral and "wrong" factual beliefs and, more generally, between moral and factual categories. Furthermore, as children appraise other persons' decisions and behaviors, they may or may not recognize that those persons proceed from beliefs different from their own and may or may not make allowances in their judgments for those different beliefs. Whether children do that (and how they do that) is likely to be informed, at least in part, by their own understandings of what beliefs are and of why people come up with diverse beliefs. By examining how children understand and evaluate those who proceed from beliefs different from their own, we are also afforded the opportunity to observe how children's developing theories of mind and epistemological understandings function in the role of factual beliefs and inform their moral thinking (Chandler, Sokol, and Wainryb, 2000).

A common assumption of those studying the development of conceptions of knowledge and epistemological understandings has been that prior to middle childhood, and in some accounts even up to their adolescent years, children are generally intolerant of diversity of belief (for a review, see Hofer and Pintrich, 1997). However, theory-of-mind researchers have recently documented a number of achievements in young children's understandings of the workings of the mind that suggest otherwise (Chandler and Lalonde, 1996; Perner, 1991; Wellman, 1990). One such development is the emergence, by the age of four or five, of the understanding that persons who have access to different information are likely to end up with different (though, in children's view, still false) beliefs. At around the age of seven or eight, children begin developing the understanding that persons might form different beliefs even when they have equal access to the relevant information; it is at this time that children begin thinking about beliefs different from their own not as necessarily false or mistaken, but as alternative interpretations of reality.

While informative regarding children's developing understandings of other people's beliefs, until very recently this research paid little attention to the domain specificity of children's understandings. The few studies that delved into the question of domain specificity (Flavell, Flavell, Green, and Moses, 1990; Flavell, Mumme, Green, and Flavell, 1992; Mansfield and Clinchy, 1993, 1997) contrasted factual beliefs, typically restricted to matters that are easily perceptible and verifiable, and value beliefs, restricted to arbitrary matters with no bearing on truth or rightness. The assumption guiding those comparisons was that factual beliefs refer to evidence grounded in the external world and value beliefs, thought to be more akin to desires, are subjective and require no extrinsic justification.

The domain-specific perspective, which has devoted more systematic attention to establishing domain distinctions on the basis of epistemological definitions and empirical evidence, strongly suggests that the distinction between a realm of values and a realm of facts is not as straightforward as it might seem. The realm of values, it has been demonstrated, encompasses more than arbitrary and subjective matters akin to desires. Research from the domain-specific perspective has documented the systematic differences that children draw in their thinking about morality (dealing with what is right and fair), convention (dealing with what is conventionally appropriate within social systems), and the personal (dealing with matters of taste and preference). Directly relevant to our purposes is the finding that children think of the personal as subjective and under the exclusive jurisdiction of the individual, but they view morality and convention as being outside the person's jurisdiction and as prescriptive either across or within contexts (Smetana, 1995; Turiel, 1998). Although there is comparatively little research concerning the specificity of children's thinking about facts, most agree that an exclusive focus on verifiable matters of fact is overly narrow. Findings from recent research suggest that children make systematic distinctions among various types of facts and that factual beliefs follow distinct developmental paths (Chandler, Sokol, and Hallett, 2001; Hallett, Chandler, and Krettenauer, 2002; Kalish, 2000). Altogether, this body of findings suggests that the age-related changes in young children's thinking about diversity of belief might be constrained in domain-specific ways. We therefore set out to examine how children think about diversity in different realms of fact and value beliefs.

In one study (Wainryb and others, forthcoming), we asked participants (ages five, seven, and nine) to consider a series of beliefs different from their own bearing on morality, taste, easily perceptible facts, and ambiguous facts. In another study (Wainryb, Shaw, Laupa, and Smith, 2001), we asked participants (ages nine, thirteen, and twenty-two) to consider diverse beliefs bearing on matters of morality, convention, religion, and psychology. Our findings indicated that five-year-old children had no difficulty considering that the characters depicted in the research stimuli held beliefs different from their own. However, children's judgments of diversity of belief were quite negative. The majority of five-year-old participants thought that each realm of belief (including matters of taste) supported only one right belief and, for the most part, judged that it was unacceptable for people to hold beliefs different from their own. These findings are consistent with the false-belief conception of the mind predicted on the basis of theory-of-mind findings, as well as with domain-specific findings showing that children, prior to the age of six or seven, have a marked difficulty grasping the relative and arbitrary nature of conventional and personal concerns and a tendency to overextend the obligatoriness and prescriptiveness of moral concepts to the conventional and personal realms (Smetana, 1981; Smetana and Braeges, 1990; Smetana, Schlagman, and Adams, 1993).

Starting at the age of seven, our findings showed, children begin recognizing the relative and subjective nature of beliefs. Although in general they make more accepting judgments of diversity of belief, their judgments are systematically constrained by the realm of diversity. Starting at the age of seven, participants distinguished consistently between diversity in moral beliefs and diversity in other realms of belief. With regard to moral diversity, they thought that there are right and wrong moral beliefs that can be identified according to prescriptive normative criteria and that it is unacceptable for people to hold the wrong moral beliefs. Even college students who, according to some accounts of epistemological development, might have been expected to be uniformly tolerant of diversity of belief, declared variation in moral beliefs to be both undesirable and unacceptable. At the same time, most participants age seven and older thought that diversity in realms of belief other than morality was acceptable. They did not, however, state that all knowledge is relative and there are no true or right answers; on the contrary, their conception of knowledge was decidedly domain specific. They systematically distinguished between realms of belief (for example, taste, ambiguous facts, religious beliefs) that are subjective and relative and realms (for example, verifiable facts, psychological beliefs) that support a single unequivocal right answer. However, they judged that wrong or mistaken beliefs in nonmoral realms, unlike wrong moral beliefs, should be tolerated.

This pattern of findings suggested that when faced with persons who engage in seemingly harmful or unjust behavior because they are acting on different beliefs, children might attend in systematic ways to those beliefs. The finding that children do not view moral beliefs different from their own as acceptable suggests that they are also not likely to think it acceptable for persons to engage in seemingly harmful behaviors on the basis of different moral beliefs. Yet the finding that children are tolerant of other (nonmoral) beliefs with which they disagree does not imply that they would necessarily think it acceptable for persons to engage in seemingly harmful behaviors because they are proceeding from those different beliefs. To examine these issues directly, we conducted a series of studies in which we told participants (ages three through twenty-one) about characters who engaged in seemingly harmful behaviors because of either moral or factual beliefs different from the participants' beliefs (baseline assessments were used to ascertain that participants thought that the depicted behaviors were harmful and that the underlying moral or factual beliefs were wrong or untrue).

In a study with three-, five-, and seven-year-old participants (Wainryb and Ford, 1998), we found that three year olds did not understand that the characters depicted in the stimuli had beliefs different from their own (even when they were explicitly and repeatedly told about it), and they uniformly evaluated the characters' behaviors in accord with their own beliefs. By comparison, five and seven year olds had little difficulty attributing to characters factual and moral beliefs different from their own. However, not all five and seven year olds considered that the characters' seemingly harmful behaviors may be justified in the light of their different factual beliefs; in fact, nearly half judged the characters' behaviors in accord with their own factual beliefs. But even when they understood that characters were acting on the basis of different moral beliefs, most five and seven year olds judged behaviors based on wrong moral beliefs to be wrong.

Starting at about the age of eight or nine, participants attended to other persons' beliefs when judging the seemingly harmful practices those persons engaged in, but they accounted differently for moral and factual beliefs. In general, they made negative judgments of practices that were based on moral beliefs different from their own but were more accepting of the same practices if they were based on factual beliefs different from their own. For example, in one study (Wainryb, 1993), children and adolescents ages eleven through twenty-one negatively judged the practice of a culture where people beat their children with sticks because they believe that it is all right to hurt children (a moral belief with which participants disagreed) but judged less negatively the same practice in a culture where people believe that children who misbehave are possessed by evil spirits that can only be exorcised with such beatings (a factual belief with which they disagreed). Their reasoning was that people who beat their children because they have a different factual understanding of what causes misbehavior are well intentioned; some also suggested that the children themselves might experience the beating as less hostile or more helpful (see also Wainryb, Shaw, and Maianu, 1998).

When taken as a whole, these findings serve to illustrate how children's developing theories of mind function in this context as a set of factual beliefs and understandings (for example, about how the mind in fact works) that inform and constrain in systematic ways children's moral judgments. Three year olds, who do not yet understand beliefs as representations of reality or conceive of people as proceeding on the basis of different beliefs, make judgments on the basis of the only understanding of reality they can conceive of: their own. Five year olds understand that persons can form "false beliefs" and often disallow those false beliefs and make judgments based on their own "true" beliefs. Somewhere between the ages of seven and nine, informed by a more mature understanding of belief and interpretation, children seem to grasp that whatever persons believe to be true (whether accurate or not) informs their moral decisions and behaviors and make fairly forgiving judgments of persons who proceeded on the basis of false factual beliefs. Recall, however, that in stark contrast to their increasingly accepting and forgiving view of those acting on different factual beliefs, children uniformly rejected those acting on wrong moral beliefs. This finding, which was consistent across studies, strongly suggests that the epistemological distinction we have proposed between moral and factual categories is echoed in children's thinking.

Do children also distinguish among different types of factual beliefs? Recall that in elaborating on our proposition about the bearing of fact beliefs on moral thinking, we acknowledged that the factual beliefs that inform moral decisions may be accurate, different but reasonable interpretations, mistaken, or mistaken in a self-serving or self-preserving way. Do children distinguish among, and are they differently forgiving of, such distinct "factual flavors"? Evidence from one of our studies (Shaw and Wainryb, 1999) indirectly suggests that college students draw distinctions, in their judgments, between factual misconstruals that are merely mistaken and those that are disingenuous and self-serving. Findings from a number of ongoing research programs examining the distinctions drawn by children among different types of facts (Chandler, Sokol, and Hallett, 2001; Hallett, Chandler, and Krettenauer, 2002; Kalish, 2000) are likely to further our understanding of children's views of different types of factual construals and misconstruals and ultimately of the ways in which different factual beliefs are integrated into children's moral thinking.

Altogether, our findings indicate that by middle childhood, children have fairly sophisticated understandings of the bearing of factual beliefs on moral decisions and make discriminating judgments about other persons' decisions and behaviors. These mature- and discerning-looking understandings are quite striking, even if we considered them within the particular conditions we have specified in our research. Recall that in our studies, participants were always told explicitly what the "other persons" believed to be factually true (for example, "those people believe that children who misbehave are possessed by evil spirits that can only be exorcised with beatings") or morally right (for example, "those people believe that it is all right to hurt children"). Those beliefs were systematically crafted and parsed out so that they would represent prototypical instances of factual or moral beliefs, and the "other persons" were hypothetical characters about whom the participants had no additional knowledge. It is possible that children's understandings and judgments might be different under different conditions. Evidence from social-psychological research with adults, for example, indicates that in the absence of explicit information about what other people think, adults tend to underestimate the extent to which other persons proceed from factual beliefs different from their own and instead tend to assume that other people proceed from different moral beliefs (Ross and Ward, 1996).

As is often the case, additional research is needed to more fully understand children's tolerance of diversity (or how they go about identifying the bad guys) under different conditions. For the purpose of understanding the relation of "is" and "ought," the findings indicate fairly clearly that at least by the age of five, children themselves make systematic distinctions between moral and factual categories that are consistent with the epistemological distinctions we have proposed, and a few years later children have a grasp of the ways in which factual beliefs inform moral decisions. These findings also illustrate how children's moral evaluations of diversity of belief—their tolerance and acceptance of different beliefs, people, and practices—are informed and constrained by their own (more or less mature, more or less accurate) understandings of the facts of the mind.

Concluding Thoughts

The injunction against going from "is" to "ought" is fundamental to our view of morality no less than it has been to Kohlberg's and other nonrelativistic approaches to morality. Ours is a proposition not about how moral concepts are derived from factual understandings of reality, but about how they are applied against a background of factual understandings of reality.

In Kohlberg's developmental account, it is clear that immature moral judgments are contingent on diverse beliefs about matters of fact, such as existing laws, norms, or expectations. The role that Kohlberg attributed to beliefs about matters of fact in relation to prescriptive moral concepts was less clear. It is possible that Kohlberg may have viewed the diversity and inconsistencies that necessarily ensue from beliefs about matters of fact as being incompatible with the prescriptivity and universality of mature morality. But perhaps he did not.

In the domain-specific model, diversity and inconsistencies are part and parcel of moral thinking (Turiel, Hildebrandt, and Wainryb, 1991; Wainryb, 1991, 1993, 2000; Wainryb and Turiel, 1993); in our interpretation, the criteria of obligatoriness and universality are meant to apply to moral concepts in their abstract manifestations (Turiel, Killen, and Helwig,

1987). Factual beliefs are part of the psychological reality that is implicated throughout development in the application of moral concepts. Within our framework, therefore, the consistent relation of "ought" and "is" cannot be overlooked. In this chapter, we have presented evidence in support of our proposition that factual beliefs about the way the world is inform and constrain moral thinking in fundamental ways; indeed, the interplay of factual beliefs and moral concepts occupies a prominent role in our explanations of moral diversity. We have also shown that fairly early on, children develop an understanding of the interplay of factual beliefs and moral decisions; their understandings of this interplay occupy a prominent role in our explanations of children's developing understandings and tolerance of moral diversity. Altogether, research into the ways in which factual understandings of reality bear on moral thinking can afford us a richer and more adequate understanding of moral development within cultures, as persons across the world can make moral judgments only about the world as they understand it to be (Turiel, 2002; Turiel and Wainryb, 2000).

References

Anscombe, G.E.M. *Ethics, Religion, and Politics.* Minneapolis: University of Minnesota Press, 1981.

Asch, S. E. *Social Psychology.* Upper Saddle River, N.J.: Prentice Hall, 1952.

Bandura, A. "Social Cognitive Theory of Moral Thought and Action." In W. M. Kurtines and J. L. Gewirtz (eds.), *Handbook of Moral Behavior and Development,* Vol. 1: *Theory.* Mahwah, N.J.: Erlbaum, 1991.

Chandler, M. J., and Lalonde, C. "Shifting to an Interpretive Theory of Mind." In A. Sameroff and M. Haith (eds.), *Reason and Responsibility: The Passage Through Childhood.* Chicago: University of Chicago Press, 1996.

Chandler, M. J., Sokol, B. W., and Hallett, D. "Moral Responsibility and the Interpretive Turn: Children's Changing Conceptions of Truth and Rightness." In B. F. Malle, L. J. Moses, and D. A. Baldwin (eds.), *Intentions and Intentionality: Foundations of Social Cognition.* Cambridge, Mass.: MIT Press, 2001.

Chandler, M. J., Sokol, B. W., and Wainryb, C. "Beliefs About Truth and Beliefs About Rightness." *Child Development,* 2000, 71, 91–97.

Duncker, K. "Ethical Relativity? An Inquiry into the Psychology of Ethics." *Mind,* 1939, 48, 39–57.

Dworkin, R. M. *A Matter of Principle.* Cambridge, Mass.: Harvard University Press, 1985.

Flavell, J. H., Flavell, E. R., Green, F. L., and Moses, L. J. "Young Children's Understanding of Fact Beliefs versus Value Beliefs." *Child Development,* 1990, 61, 915–928.

Flavell, J. H., Mumme, D. L., Green, F. L., and Flavell, E. R. "Young Children's Understanding of Different Types of Beliefs." *Child Development,* 1992, 63, 960–977.

Frankena, W. K. *Ethics.* Upper Saddle River, N.J.: Prentice Hall, 1973.

Hallett, D., Chandler, M. J., and Krettenauer, T. "Disentangling the Course of Epistemic Development: Parsing Knowledge by Epistemic Content." *New Ideas in Psychology,* 2002, 20, 285–307.

Hare, R. M. *The Language of Morals.* New York: Oxford University Press, 1952.

Hofer, B. K., and Pintrich, P. R. "The Development of Epistemological Theories: Beliefs About Knowledge and Knowing and Their Relation to Learning." *Review of Educational Research,* 1997, 67(1), 88–140.

Hume, D. *A Treatise of Human Nature* (L. A. Selby-Bigge and P. H. Nidditch, eds.). (2nd ed.) New York: Oxford University Press, 1978. (Originally published 1739.)

Kalish, C. "Children's Thinking About Truth: A Parallel to Social Domain Judgments?" In M. Laupa (ed.), *Rights and Wrongs: How Children and Young Adults Evaluate the World.* New Directions for Child and Adolescent Development, no. 89. San Francisco: Jossey-Bass, 2000.

Kohlberg, L. "From Is to Ought: How to Commit the Naturalistic Fallacy and Get Away with It in the Study of Moral Development." In T. Mischel (ed.), *Cognitive Development and Epistemology.* Orlando, Fla.: Academic Press, 1971.

Kohlberg, L. *The Philosophy of Moral Development: Moral Stages and the Idea of Justice.* San Francisco: Harper San Francisco, 1981.

Kohlberg, L., and Elfenbein, D. "Moral Judgments About Capital Punishment: A Developmental-Psychological View." In H. A. Bedan and C. M. Pierce (eds.), *Capital Punishment in the United States.* New York: AMS Press, 1976.

MacIntyre, A. C. *After Virtue: A Study in Moral Theory.* Notre Dame, Ind.: University of Notre Dame Press, 1984.

Mansfield, A., and Clinchy, B. M. "Continuity and Change in Children's Epistemologies from Age Four to Ten." Paper presented at the Biennial Meeting of the Society for Research in Child Development, New Orleans, La., Apr. 1993.

Mansfield, A., and Clinchy, B. M. "Toward the Integration of Objectivity and Subjectivity: A Longitudinal Study of Epistemological Development Between the Ages of Nine and Twelve." Paper presented at the Biennial Meeting of the Society for Research in Child Development, Washington, D.C., Apr. 1997.

Nucci, L., and Lee, J. "Morality and Personal Autonomy." In G. G. Noam, T. E. Wren, G. Nunner-Winkler, and W. Edelstein (eds.), *The Moral Self.* Cambridge, Mass.: MIT Press, 1993.

Perner, J. *Understanding the Representational Mind.* Cambridge, Mass.: MIT Press, 1991.

Putnam, H. *The Many Faces of Realism.* LaSalle, Ill.: Open Court, 1987.

Rawls, J. *A Theory of Justice.* Cambridge, Mass.: Belknap Press, 1971.

Ross, L., and Ward, A. "Naive Realism in Everyday Life: Implications for Social Conflict and Disagreement." In E. S. Reed, E. Turiel, and T. Brown (eds.), *Values and Knowledge.* Mahwah, N.J.: Erlbaum, 1996.

Shaw, L. A., and Wainryb, C. "The Outsider's Perspective: Young Adults' Judgments of Social Practices of Other Cultures." *British Journal of Developmental Psychology,* 1999, *17,* 451–471.

Smetana, J. G. "Preschool Children's Conceptions of Moral and Social Rules." *Child Development,* 1981, *52,* 1333–1336.

Smetana, J. G. "Morality in Context: Abstractions, Ambiguities, and Applications." In R. Vasta (ed.), *Annals of Child Development.* London: Jessica Kingsley, 1995.

Smetana, J. G., and Braeges, J. "The Development of Toddlers' Moral and Conventional Judgments." *Merrill-Palmer Quarterly,* 1990, *36,* 329–346.

Smetana, J. G., Schlagman, N., and Adams, P. W. "Preschool Children's Judgments About Hypothetical and Actual Transgressions." *Child Development,* 1993, *64,* 202–214.

Turiel, E. *The Development of Social Knowledge: Morality and Convention.* Cambridge: Cambridge University Press, 1983.

Turiel, E. "The Development of Morality." In W. Damon (series ed.) and N. Eisenberg (vol. ed.), *Handbook of Child Psychology,* Vol. 3: *Social, Emotional, and Personality Development.* (5th ed.) New York: Wiley, 1998.

Turiel, E. *The Culture of Morality: Social Development, Context, and Conflict.* Cambridge: Cambridge University Press, 2002.

Turiel, E., Hildebrandt, C., and Wainryb, C. "Judging Social Issues: Difficulties, Inconsistencies, and Consistencies." *Monographs of the Society for Research in Child Development,* 1991, *56* (2, serial no. 224).

Turiel, E., Killen, M., and Helwig, C. "Morality: Its Structure, Functions, and Vagaries." In J. Kagan and S. Lamb (eds.), *The Emergence of Morality in Young Children*. Chicago: University of Chicago Press, 1987.

Turiel, E., and Wainryb, C. "Social Life in Cultures: Judgments, Conflict, and Subversion." *Child Development*, 2000, 71, 250–256.

Wainryb, C. "Understanding Differences in Moral Judgments: The Role of Informational Assumptions." *Child Development*, 1991, 62, 840–851.

Wainryb, C. "The Application of Moral Judgments to Other Cultures: Relativism and Universality." *Child Development*, 1993, 64, 924–933.

Wainryb, C. "Values and Truths: The Making and Judging of Moral Decisions." In M. Laupa (ed.), *Rights and Wrongs: How Children and Young Adults Evaluate the World*. New Directions for Child and Adolescent Development, no. 89. San Francisco: Jossey-Bass, 2000.

Wainryb, C., and Ford, S. "Young Children's Evaluations of Acts Based on Beliefs Different from Their Own." *Merrill-Palmer Quarterly*, 1998, 44, 484–503.

Wainryb, C., and Laupa, M. "Moral and Informational Components in Social Decision-Making: Young Adults' Reasoning about Capital Punishment." Poster presented at the twenty-fourth meeting of the Jean Piaget Society, Chicago, June 1994.

Wainryb, C., and others. "Children's Thinking About Diversity of Belief in the Early School Years: Judgments of Relativism, Tolerance, and Disagreeing Persons." *Child Development*, forthcoming.

Wainryb, C., Shaw, L. A., Laupa, M., and Smith, K. "Children's, Adolescents', and Young Adults' Thinking About Different Types of Disagreements." *Developmental Psychology*, 2001, 37, 373–386.

Wainryb, C., Shaw, L. A., and Maianu, C. "Tolerance and Intolerance: Children's and Adolescents' Judgments of Dissenting Beliefs, Speech, Persons, and Conduct." *Child Development*, 1998, 69, 1541–1555.

Wainryb, C., and Turiel, E. "Conceptual and Informational Features in Moral Decision Making." *Educational Psychologist*, 1993, 28, 205–218.

Wellman, H. M. *The Child's Theory of Mind*. Cambridge, Mass.: MIT Press, 1990.

Wertheimer, M. "Some Problems in the Theory of Ethics." *Social Research*, 1935, 2, 353–367.

CECILIA WAINRYB *is associate professor of psychology at the University of Utah.*

2

The authors criticize the central place of belief-desire psychology in the theories-of-mind enterprise. They detail the merits of adopting a more agentive framework for conceptualizing human action and demonstrate how children's growing understanding of epistemic agency relates to advances in moral reasoning.

From Mechanical to Autonomous Agency: The Relationship Between Children's Moral Judgments and Their Developing Theories of Mind

Bryan W. Sokol, Michael J. Chandler, Christopher Jones

Despite their linchpin role in the ordinary self-understanding of ordinary people, familiar notions of human agency, the central stuff of this chapter, have never succeeded in finding a workable place in the traditional explanatory armamentarium of psychology. Within recent memory, even the slightest whiff of agentiveness was enough to evoke the discipline's signature fear of vitalism (Skinner, 1973), the very thing that psychology as a science had arisen to defeat. While this reflexive aversion to all talk of human agency is perhaps less automatic than was once the case, remnants of this persistent squeamishness are not altogether missing. For many, the problem is set by Wittgenstein's famous question: "What is left over if I subtract the fact that my arm goes up from the fact that I raise my arm?" This curious arithmetic is usually seen to yield two kinds of phenomena. The first, historically ceded to philosophy, has to do with all those human activities that are guided by so-called higher faculties, such as beliefs or intentions. Such purposeful *actions*, as they are commonly identified, are generally construed as agentive in nature and held in contrast to lesser, nonagentive *behaviors*. This second

---

The research presented in this chapter was supported by a doctoral fellowship to the first author from the Natural Science and Engineering Research Council of Canada (NSERC) and an NSERC operating grant to the second author. We are grateful to the children, parents, teachers, and staff who participated in these studies. Special thanks also go to Tracey Burns and David Paul for their help collecting data.

category, taken up as psychology's proper subject matter, is meant to capture all the remaining occurrences or happenings that are passively registered in human bodies. Although this subtract-and-conquer strategy has very long legs, there is anything but consensus about whether such a division of labor is the best way to achieve conceptual clarity concerning the more constitutive dimensions of agency. Even Wittgenstein himself (see Hacker, 1996) seemed unsatisfied with this either-or distinction between actions and behaviors, and in more contemporary circles, there are several (for example, Frankfurt, 1988, and Velleman, 2000) who have argued that expanding the number of categories from just two to three is a necessary step toward adequate self-understanding. Alternatively, there are also those who, moving in the opposite direction, have tried to reduce the whole of human behavior to just one foundational category, a flatland in which all dated talk of "agency" is relegated to the dustbin of superstition (Churchland, 1984). Clearly, anyone in search of guidance about the proper place of agency in contemporary psychological thought will find anything but unambiguous directions by consulting the available philosophical charts.

The particular tack that we take up in our own search for some better way of thinking about agentiveness has less to do with choosing sides in this debate than with appropriating the language that surrounds it in an effort to draw out and clarify a critical issue in the runaway literature on children's developing theories of mind. Specifically, we will argue that in its push to characterize how children construct folk psychological laws of human action by inferring others' beliefs and desires (Gopnik and Wellman, 1994), the theories-of-mind enterprise has inadvertently promoted an impoverished conception of agency that, in the end, proves to be incompatible with day-to-day conceptions of mind and morality. We contend that if efforts, such as those contained in this volume, are to succeed in building a connective bridge between theories-of-mind research and the field of sociomoral development, then adequately addressing the problem of human agency must become one of the central tasks of those working in the area. Our contribution here is meant as a sketch for a blueprint of this larger constructive effort.

The first section of this chapter is a critical examination of the widespread assumption, particularly virulent among those most associated with the theories-of-mind enterprise, that human actions are governed by an individual's desires and beliefs. This view is clear, for instance, in Wellman's widely circulated description of belief-desire psychology (1990) as providing the necessary organizing principles for understanding children's early conceptions of mind. It is also well represented in Kim's influential text, *Philosophy of Mind* (1996), where he states quite explicitly that "it seems essential to our concept of action that our bodies are moved in appropriate ways by our wants and beliefs" (p. 8). As it turns out, these are only some of the more recent expressions of a view whose intellectual history stretches at least as far back as the empiricist philosophies of Hobbes (see his

Leviathan, Part 1, Chapter 6) and Hume (*A Treatise of Human Nature;* see McNaughton, 1988). In fact, this historical note proves significant, since it is the mechanistic conceptual baggage inherent in empiricist worldviews (see Overton, 1991), and carried along by belief-desire psychology, that becomes the main sticking point in our discussion of agency and its relationship to morality.

The second section of the chapter is more data driven. It represents our initial efforts to step outside the usual belief-desire framework and make room for a richer conception of human agency. We argue that because the standard "unexpected transfer" procedure (Wimmer and Perner, 1983) for measuring children's understanding of false-belief formation tacitly presupposes the mind's passive accommodation to the effects of the external world, the data it generates can provide us with only a partial story of how young people conceive of agency. In elaborating this claim, we mean to capitalize on previous research exploring children's transition to an interpretive theory of mind (Carpendale and Chandler, 1996; Chandler and Lalonde, 1996; Lalonde and Chandler, 2002) and to describe how this more active conception of mental life serves as a marker for other advances in children's notions about intentional action and moral responsibility (Chandler, Sokol, and Hallett, 2001; Sokol, Jones, Paul, and Chandler, 2000).

The Hydraulics of Human Action

It is common practice in the theories-of-mind literature to refer to beliefs and desires as contrasting mental states (Astington and Gopnik, 1991) that differ according to opposing directions of fit between the mind and the world. Trading on language popularized by Searle (1983), beliefs are said to fit with the world, relating to it by reproducing or re-presenting the world's contents inside the mind. Desires, by contrast, reverse this relationship; instead of representing things as they currently stand, they work to transform the world to how one wishes it to be—that is, by having the world fit with the ambitions of the mind. On this account, it should be clear that beliefs are taken to serve as the quintessential representational state, while desires perform a more motivational function. This fundamental contrast is perhaps most evident in the distinct roles that these mental states are said to play in explanations of human action. That is, desires are typically seen as providing the motive force, or hydraulic push, that drives behavior, and beliefs are taken as supplying the information that properly channels, or guides, this force (see, for example, Harris and others, 1989). Beliefs, as McNaughton (1988) has noted, are "motivationally inert; they are merely passive responses to the way the world is" (p. 107); desires "are active; directed as they are towards obtaining something, they are intrinsically 'pushy'" (p. 107). On the face of it, there is certainly a great deal of intuitive appeal to this model of action, or belief-desire psychology. Still, the "hydraulic metaphor" underlying this definition of beliefs and desires (McNaughton, 1988) carries with it some inherent difficulties for those who might attempt to transport such a model into the domain of moral agency.

In a nutshell, the problem with belief-desire psychology is that it too easily allows human action to be construed as the mechanized output of what Harré (1982) has called "subpersonal components" in the agent's mind. With these isolated parts now taking center stage in action-explanations, the integrative role of the agent or person, to which any such component beliefs and desires are said to belong, is reduced to that of a bit player and effectively explained away. Having said this, we do not want to be misunderstood as implying that the attribution of beliefs and desires, as part of everyday action-explanations, is a mistake. Adults and children do quite regularly apply such mental states in their accounts of behavior and no doubt use them to reasonably explain and predict others' actions. Rather, our dispute arises when these loosely held notions of "explain" and "predict" become tied to the mechanistic or empiricist language of the physical sciences and instead are taken to mean "cause" and "determine." The result is to strip the individual of any real agentive abilities, leaving instead a hollowed-out shell that, as Velleman (1993) has argued, serves "merely as the arena for these [mental] events" (p. 189).

The overall posture of the current theories-of-mind literature sets up the conditions for just this kind of slippage. That is, by adopting the widely held view that beliefs and desires are analogous to "theoretical constructs" (Perner, 1991, p. 108) that "provide *causal* explanations" (Gopnik and Wellman, 1994, p. 260, emphasis added) for others' behavior, it is all too easy to slip into making claims such as that it is "what actors think—their representation of the world. . . . [that] inevitably *determines* their actions" (Gopnik and Wellman, 1994, p. 264, emphasis added), or, even worse, into imagining that a simple "practical syllogism . . . works if no unusual circumstances intervene" (Perner, 1991, p. 108) to establish a psychological law (for example, "If Homer wants the beer and thinks it is in the fridge, then he will go there") that is adequate enough to capture the essence of human action. Such a privileging of impersonal, causal language to describe everyday experience has been characterized by Dewey (1989) as the very sort of "intellectualism" that, when allowed to proceed unchecked (as it has been in the theories-of-mind literature), wrongly supplants our primary experience of agency as the basis for understanding human action. As a result, we are left, in Campbell's (1995) words, with a "fragmented. . . . picture of human action that fits a machine better than an organism" (p. 34).

Similar early warning bells can be heard in the two-century-old cautionary remarks of the Enlightenment philosopher Thomas Reid (1863). He argued, in particular, that though "we reason from men's motives [that is, their beliefs and desires] to their actions, and, in many cases, with great probability," we never do so "with absolute certainty" (p. 612). This is because human actions are not simply logical outcomes that follow necessarily from the identification of some belief-desire combination. That is, although people may generally acknowledge, as recent research by Malle (1999) suggests, that beliefs and desires constitute "an agent's reasons for choosing to act a certain way" (p. 24), they are not, by themselves, "an empirically sufficient condition for the performance of the action" (Hacker, 1996, p. 581). Rather, actions are widely understood, at least among everyday folk, to be the natural purview of agents—or persons—who demonstrate self-motivation and exert self-control. An agent's reasons, in other words, must be set apart from the language of mere causes (Chandler, Lalonde, and Sokol, 1998; see also Heider, 1958; Malle, 1999).

If we are willing to grant this, then it becomes necessary to rework the standard practice by which belief-desire psychology is applied to folk conceptions of action. More specifically, we must allow for an account that as Duff (1990) has suggested, sees "persons and actions . . . [as] logically *basic* categories [that] cannot be explained by an analysis which seeks to reduce them to supposedly simpler elements" (p. 130). In other words, beliefs and desires need to be reintegrated into a conceptual framework that treats human agency as the primary unit of analysis instead of something to be analyzed away.

Agency Regained

There are other voices besides our own in the contemporary theories-of-mind literature that have tried to raise this and related matters. White (1995), for instance, has noted a "curious omission" (p. 68) in many studies where, with all the emphasis placed on children's notions of belief or desire, very little consideration is given to "children's understanding of the person whose mental states and representations they are" (p. 69). Hobson (1993) has similarly argued that by maintaining the classic dualism between mind and matter, the theories-of-mind enterprise, as it now stands, fails to recognize that "the concept of 'persons' is more fundamental than either the concept of 'bodies' or the concept of 'minds'" (p. 115). Finally, Blasi (1995) has suggested that current cognitive psychology, as a whole, will continue to neglect the significance of human agency until it recovers "the idea that knowledge belongs to, [and] is an intrinsic possession of the conscious person, who intentionally pursues it and is responsible for its correctness and truth" (p. 235).

For our own part, sorting out the various stances that one might take toward human agency has proven indispensable in our ongoing investigations of children's emerging conceptions of the epistemic, or knowing, process. The bulk of these empirical efforts (Carpendale and Chandler, 1996; Lalonde and Chandler, 2002) has focused on the question of representational diversity and whether, in particular, children's success on standard false-belief measures should be equated, as some have claimed (see, for example, Meltzoff and Gopnik, 1993; Perner, 1991; Wellman, 1990), with an appreciation of the fact that individuals may hold multiple interpretations of reality. We have argued (Chandler and Sokol, 1999) that such a rich interpretation of children's abilities is unwarranted. Nothing we say here will change that. Still, because it may be easy to miss how questions of agency are implicated in this earlier work, what we mean to review about these matters in the rest of the chapter narrows in on how matters of interpretation are naturally wedded to human agentiveness. Specifically, our emphasis will be on the distinction that has been drawn between a copy theory and an interpretive theory of mind (Chandler and Boyes, 1982; Wellman, 1990) and, more particularly, the implicit conceptions of epistemic agency that each carries. If, in the end, our analysis is to be convincing, then not only should these different "theories" have measurable consequences for children's views about morality and intentionality, but it should also help to make clear why belief-desire psychology, at least as it is commonly conceived in theories-of-mind research, fails to adequately capture the dramatic changes that the typical five to seven year old experiences in thinking about mental life.

Mental "Activities." One of the more generally accepted claims in theories-of-mind research is that young children are first committed to a "causal," or passive (Pillow, 1988, 1995) conception of the knowing process. By this account, young persons first begin the epistemic enterprise by effectively treating their own and others' minds as "passive recorders" that simply "bear the scars of information which has been imbossed upon them" by the external world (Chandler and Boyes, 1982, p. 391). Such a copy theory of mind, we would argue, naturally leads children to view epistemic agency as originating outside, or external to, the individual (see also Bickhard, 1980). In other words, from this initial point in children's understanding of epistemic life, the mind's activity is not its own (see Wellman and Hickling, 1994); rather, it is merely the mechanical response to causal forces beyond the subject's control. Referring back to the language of Wittgenstein and other action-theorists, mental life here is little more than a series of occurrences or happenings that, despite making one's mind an arena of activity (the place where such occurrences are housed), leaves out any real action on the part of an autonomous agent. In truth, for the young copy-theorist, an epistemic "patient" stands in place of the so-called knowing agent.

By contrast, when children come to hold an interpretive view of the knowing process, they relinquish their earlier causal conceptions of the mind in favor of a more fully agentive understanding of mental life. This particular transition is characterized not by how children see the mind as passively accommodating to the impact of the world, but by how it actively transforms or interprets the world to better assimilate experience to its existing knowledge structures. By this interpretive account, then, the epistemic process is viewed as consisting of both a passive and an active dimension. That is, there are simultaneously the "objective" uptake of information from the world and the "subjective" attempt to give it meaning. Most important for our purposes here, though, is the fact that children holding such an interpretive theory of mind no longer view the knowing process as just another instance of what some might call "mechanical agency" (Bandura, 1986, p. 12). Rather, they attribute the mind's activity to an "autonomous agent" who not only reacts to the world but also actively tries to make sense of it.

The different forms of agency associated with each of these childhood conceptions of mental life formed the impetus for the empirical work to be reported here. More specifically, the brace of studies we describe are meant to help demonstrate the particular shift in sociomoral outlook that young school-aged children experience when coming to view human persons as inherently active, or autonomous, epistemic agents (as opposed to passive mechanical agents). To this end, findings from the first study show that depending on whether they ascribe to a copy theory or interpretive theory of mind, children take sharply diverging approaches in their evaluations of others' moral actions. In short, interpretive children base their judgments almost entirely on the plans or intentions assumed to underlie particular acts. Noninterpretive children, by contrast, place much less emphasis on such motivational considerations. The second study follows up on these results by more closely investigating children's conceptions of action motivation and whether, in particular, actions are viewed as the passive results of simple desires or the more active consequences of carefully formulated intentions. As these data show, only children holding to an interpretive theory of mind appreciate the important conceptual distinction that divides these differing motivational states. Before explaining any of these details further, however, it is essential to clarify just what an interpretive theory of mind looks like in young children and, more important, why a simple appreciation of false belief falls significantly short of an interpretive achievement.

False Beliefs About False Belief. To illustrate this critical difference, consider how the typical scenario used to measure children's understanding of false belief amounts to little more than a twist on the old cliché: "seeing is believing." In Wimmer and Perner's now classic "unexpected transfer" task (1983), a puppet character, Maxi, is out of the room when, unbeknown to him, his chocolate bar is taken from the cupboard where he put it and left in another place. Child participants in this task who are old enough to appreciate that a person has to at least "see" an event occur in order to know something about it, and who are equally capable of reversing this logic by recognizing that "not seeing" has the consequence of leaving one ignorant about particular matters, have all the cognitive prerequisites necessary for understanding what it means to hold a false belief about reality. The working definition of belief in this task is merely a matter of sorting out what aspects of reality a person has been exposed to and so has had an opportunity to register in their mind. That is, despite claims to the contrary (Perner, 1991), the Maxi task and others like it require no more than a passive copy theory of mind. By contrast, coming to appreciate that people can, and commonly do, differently interpret one and the same object or event requires (in addition to simple false belief understanding) some basic and new-found comprehension of how the knowing process is informed by an active mind-to-world contribution on the part of autonomous human agents.

As it turns out, this is precisely what previous research (Carpendale and Chandler, 1996; Chandler and Lalonde, 1996; Lalonde and Chandler, 2002) has established. In particular, this body of work demonstrates that while three or four year olds may well appreciate that those given access to different information will hold differing beliefs, it is typically not until they are seven or eight years old that such children also recognize that those having the same information can also make different interpretive sense of it. In our efforts to replace the typical false-belief procedure with a more suitable measure, we have found that children's understanding of interpretive diversity is best gauged using ambiguous visual stimuli, such as Roger Price's famous "ship-witch" droodle (1953; see Figure 2.1). The "restricted" droodle image seen in this diagram, not unlike a Rorschach inkblot, may elicit from casual observers any number of legitimate beliefs about what it really is. In the context of our experiments with young school-aged children, for instance, participants have credited various puppet observers with interpretations that diverge as dramatically as "two knife points," "sharks' teeth," and "dolphin fins," to name only a few (see Lalonde, 1997; Lalonde and Chandler, 2002). Children said to hold an interpretive theory of mind, in fact, quite readily make diverse attributions about others' beliefs in such ambiguous situations. In contrast, children holding a noninterpretive theory of mind always attribute the same belief to independent observers. That is, while such noninterpretive children may recognize that observers are ignorant about what the droodle really is (that is, they succeed at comprehending simple false belief), they nevertheless imagine that everyone will think the ambiguous image is exactly the same thing. For these young children, the formation of belief, the essence of the knowing process, is rooted in the causal push of external, "objective" reality. The mind, by default, reflects external experience even when it remains unclear. By contrast, interpretive children are found to treat the ambiguity of these drawings very differently. For them, the droodle procedure presents the ideal circumstances under which the inherent "subjective" activity of the mind can show itself, and thus, for autonomous epistemic agency to proceed unchecked. As we mean to show now, though, recognizing the autonomy of knowing agents, as interpretive children do, has still further ramifications.

Agency and Morality. Perhaps the clearest way in which matters of human agency affect our daily lives can be demonstrated by simply looking at our ordinary attempts to apportion praise and blame to others. That is, common sense tells us that only those who are perceived as active "agents," as opposed to mere "patients," can rightly be held accountable for their actions. This view is evident, for instance, in our various moral and legal

Figure 2.1. The Ship-Witch Droodle

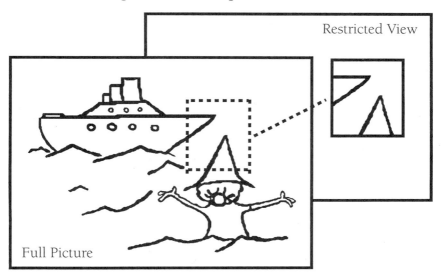

considerations. People whose trigger finger is controlled by wires or persons who, through coercion or diminished mental capacity, are not free to actively form intentions, are ordinarily excused from responsibility for their actions (see, for example, Fincham and Roberts, 1985). In contrast, those people who have engaged in cold-blooded deliberation and then followed through on their plans are generally seen to be deserving of whatever punishments our legal canons allow.

Taking all this, then, as well as what we have learned about children who either do or do not ascribe to an interpretive theory of mind, we individually interviewed nearly fifty children five to seven years old regarding their judgments of another's morally reprehensible actions (Chandler, Sokol, and Hallett, 2001; Sokol, 1998). Following a set of procedures very much like Piaget's well-known paradigm (1965) that pits intentions against consequences, the children in this study were first shown a series of slapstick films in which the classic puppet character, Punch, attempts to do in his partner, Judy, by throwing her into the trash. After each episode, children were asked to evaluate, using a five-point "badness meter," just how guilty and deserving of punishment Punch was. The results of the two "attempted murder" scenarios, in which Punch had every intention of harming Judy but inadvertently failed, are shown in Figure 2.2 for children who had been previously coded as subscribing to either a copy theory or interpretive theory of mental life. (More specific details of the story conditions and coding procedures can be found in Chandler, Sokol, and Hallett, 2001. For the most part, however, children were scored as having either a copy theory or an interpretive theory of mind based on their understanding of

Figure 2.2. Children's "Badness" Ratings of Punch in the "Attempted Murder" Scenarios

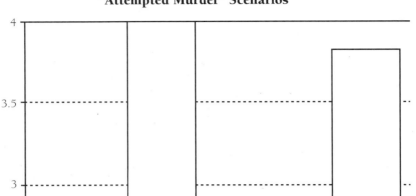

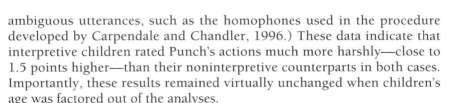

ambiguous utterances, such as the homophones used in the procedure developed by Carpendale and Chandler, 1996.) These data indicate that interpretive children rated Punch's actions much more harshly—close to 1.5 points higher—than their noninterpretive counterparts in both cases. Importantly, these results remained virtually unchanged when children's age was factored out of the analyses.

Although the diverging pattern of results for these two groups seems striking enough, the most significant detail revolves around the fact that both interpretive and noninterpretive children alike were able to respond appropriately to interview questions about Punch's subversive intentions. That is, all the children were found to understand correctly what Punch was "trying to do" and whether his thinly veiled attempt at murder was in fact "on purpose" or not. When this procedural detail is combined with other research demonstrating that even three year olds can appropriately comment on others' motivations (Chandler, Greenspan, and Barenboim, 1973; Joseph and Tager-Flusberg, 1999; Nelson, 1980), the evident differences in how interpretive and noninterpretive children register the role of agency in their moral judgments becomes a bit of a puzzle.

The key, we would argue, turns on children's early notions of intention and the crucial difference between mechanical and autonomous conceptions of agency. What remains unsettled, however, is just what a child's understanding of intention might look like from a mechanistic point of view. That is, the language surrounding intentions typically resists being mapped onto mechanistic assumptions. Certainly any talk of responsibility, at least as it is commonly understood, would make little sense if individuals were not somehow seen to have an active hand in the formation of their intentions. It seems only reasonable to ask, then, whether intentions can be made to fit outside an autonomous framework. The irony here is that an answer can be seen in the tacit assumptions guiding much of contemporary theories-of-mind research. Bringing these assumptions to the surface, then, became one of the central tasks of our follow-up study.

Desires Versus Intentions. All that we said in the first section of this chapter about efforts to reduce action to some mechanistic combination of beliefs and desires applies with equal force to our concerns about intention. That is, intentions, just like beliefs and desires, can and have been shrunk to fit within the same impersonal, empiricist framework that has dominated the theories-of-mind literature. As a result, the language being bantered about to characterize intentions has a familiar causal ring. For instance, in ways reminiscent of earlier accounts of beliefs and desires, intentions are commonly said to "*cause* the actions they represent" (Astington, 2001, p. 88, emphasis added) and to "underlie and *cause* bodily movements" (Meltzoff, Gopnik, and Repacholi, 1999, p. 24, emphasis added). The real problem with these views about intention, however, comes with what they tend to omit. That is, nothing about them suggests, as Kenny (1963) has remarked, that "an intention (in the sense of making a decision) is itself a human action" (p. 94). Our point here is that intentions are more than mere causal mental entities. Rather, they fundamentally represent an active process that is initiated by an autonomous agent. Failing to honor this division between entities and activities is perhaps justified within a system that makes mechanical agency the only live option, but this is clearly not the case for those who also take the possibility of autonomous agency seriously. The guiding thesis in our second study, then, went as follows. Children who could be credited with an interpretive theory of mind, and so also an autonomous conception of epistemic agency, would be better situated than their noninterpretive counterparts to recognize the fundamentally active underpinnings of intention. In other words, interpretive children would recognize that intentions constitute a self-initiated, or autonomous, mental activity.

To operationalize this active dimension, we turned to Bratman's characterization of human beings as fundamentally "planning agents" (1987, p. 2). According to Bratman, we recognize in ourselves not only the ability to act purposively but, more significant, as being constituted by our capacity to form and execute plans. From this view, then, although some of our actions may be described as fulfilling present-directed desires, or wants, much of what we do follows from more "future-directed" prior intentions, or plans. In other words, an individual's act of deliberation is said to distinguish prior intentions from simpler desires. As a result, even though both intentions and desires may be seen more generally as motivational attitudes, there is a great deal to suggest that collapsing them into a single category is a mistake (Astington, 2001). Specifically, intentions implicate a kind of autonomous epistemic agency that desires, by themselves, do not. In fact, desires refer only to specific outcomes or end states of actions (see Malle and Knobe, 2001) that exist quite apart from, or external to, the agent's deliberations. To say, for instance, that an individual's desires are fulfilled in no way requires that their deliberative activity be evoked as well. To illustrate, consider Searle's description of a "deviant causal chain" (1983, p. 82; see also Astington, 1993, p. 95) in which a person's desires are ultimately met, but not in the particular way in which he or she intended or planned.

According to this oft-cited philosophical example, a young man who wants to kill his rich uncle so that he can collect his inheritance carelessly drives his car over a pedestrian while being caught up in making his cold-blooded plans to shoot the uncle. The dead pedestrian, it so happens, is the young man's uncle. The young man has clearly had his desire met: the uncle is as dead as can be. Still, because the plan was to shoot his uncle, it must not be said that the young man has fulfilled his intention. This is because intentions are "self-referential" (Searle, 1983) and so, in order to be fulfilled, require that an action, or sequence of actions, occur under the description in which they were originally conceived.

As it turns out, such a deviant causal chain provides the necessary test case to investigate our hypothesis that interpretive and noninterpretive children differ in their conceptions of intention. Using a more benign version of this basic scenario, a sample of forty-five children between the ages of five and seven, who were also gauged for their interpretive theory of mind (see the droodle procedure described earlier), were individually interviewed and presented with a pair of stories containing contrasting deviant causal chains. In the first of these (story A), the protagonist's plans are left unfulfilled, but her overall goal is achieved, and so when children were asked to respond to the primary test questions of whether the story character "did what she *planned*" and "got what she *wanted*," the proper response pattern was "no" (she did not do as she planned), but "yes" (she did get what she wanted). For the second story condition (story B), precisely the opposite pattern applied. That is, children were presented with a scenario in which

Table 2.1. Intention Task Story Conditions

		Intention Satisfied	
		Yes	No
Desire Satisfied	Yes		Story A
	No	Story B	

the protagonist did in fact proceed with her plan, but nevertheless failed to obtain the desired goal. The appropriate responses to the test questions here, then, were "yes" (she did as planned) and "no" (she did not get what she wanted). Quite simply, then, these two story conditions (see Table 2.1) contrasted according to whether the character's desires or intentions were being satisfied (for a similar procedure see Schult, 1996).

To be clear, children needed to respond correctly to both the "plan" and the "want" questions in order to be scored as passing a particular condition, and so they could potentially fail both story conditions, pass just one, or successfully navigate the entire set. The results are summarized in Table 2.2. Here we see the number of conditions passed by participants who were coded as noninterpretive, transitionally interpretive, or fully interpretive in their conceptions of mental life. All of the children we tested, it should be noted, were quite adept at demonstrating their understanding of simple false belief. Still, just under two-thirds of the sample failed to respond adequately to the pair of droodle conditions making up the interpretive measure. (Those who passed only one condition constituted the transitional category.)

What these data indicate is that as the child's interpretive theory of mind develops, so too does his or her comprehension of the distinction between intentions or plans and simpler desires or wants. In fact, as we can see in Table 2.3, the correlation between successful performance on the intention task and the theory-of-mind task is quite high: $r = .57$, $p < .001$. Still, children's age or verbal intelligence (as measured by the Peabody Picture Vocabulary Test) might well account for this emerging competence. As evidenced by the .50 and .46 correlations, respectively, both of these variables are also quite useful predictors of how well children succeed in distinguishing between intentions and desires. By computing the semipartial correlations for each of these factors, however, we see in Table 2.4 that the child's theory of mind wins the race by carrying with it the most predictive power. That is, when we account for the unique variance associated with each of these factors, only the children's theory-of-mind score remains statistically significant: $r = .38$, $p < .05$.

Table 2.2. Summary of Children's Performance for Each of the Intention Task Conditions

	Failed Both	Passed One	Passed Both
Noninterpretive ($n = 12$)	4	6	2
Transitional interpretive ($n = 15$)	0	11	4
Fully interpretive ($n = 18$)	0	5	13

$\chi_2 = 21.03; p = .0003; N = 45.$

Table 2.3. Pattern of Correlations for Children's Age, Verbal Ability, and Performance on Experimental Tasks

	Age	Verbal Ability	Theory of Mind	Intention Task
Age		.61	.70	.50
Verbal ability	.61		.59	.46
Theory of mind	.70	.59		.57
Intention task	.50	.46	.57	

Note: All $p < .001$.

Table 2.4. Semipartial Correlations for the Intention Task

Predictor Variable	Semipartial Correlation	p value
Age	.15	.44
Verbal ability	.15	.38
Theory of mind	.38	.044

Conclusions

In light of these results, we can now make better sense of the children's moral judgments in the first study and argue that noninterpretive children reduced Punch's malicious intentions in the two story conditions to the status of simpler desires. As a result, they failed to give proper moral consideration to the mental activities (Punch's active deliberations) leading up to his outward attempt to do Judy harm. Instead, their more mechanistic conception of epistemic agency led them to focus on the events external to Punch's subjective mental processes. In this way, noninterpretive children may be seen to assume, as Piaget (1965) would say, an "objective" stance toward moral responsibility. Interpretive children, by contrast, were capable of taking the full epistemic measure of Punch's intentions and so could not help but recognize the weight that such mental acts should hold in their moral judgments. That is, they saw in Punch's bad intentions the active hand of an autonomous epistemic agent, who should be made to answer not only for his outward behaviors but also for his inner subjective activities. Such interpretive children, then, could be said to hold a "subjective" notion of responsibility.

The upshot that these findings have for the broader theories-of-mind enterprise is threefold. First, to be clear, despite obviously trading on Piaget's original characterization (1965) of subjective and objective responsibility, the account of children's moral reasoning we have worked to advance does not also take up the intention-consequence distinction that is typically understood to set these two views of morality apart. The dividing lines in our research are defined, rather, by the distinct forms of epistemic agency that children with either a copy theory or interpretive theory of mind are committed to holding. These children's moral judgments diverge according to the different motivating principles that they understand to be operative in the minds of moral agents. For copy theorists, these principles are largely mechanical, rooted in a passive "desire-based" conception of action, and not all seen as "belonging" to an active agent. By contrast, interpretive theorists see these principles as autonomous and emerging out of a more active, or "intention-based," framework. As a result, children who have rounded this interpretive turn now recognize that moral agents exert a kind of ownership (see Blasi, 1991, 1995; Ross, 1973; Taylor, 1963, 1966) over their thoughts and deeds that was largely absent in their earlier passive conception of epistemic life. All this made for the very different, though predictable, approaches that the children in our research took toward questions of moral responsibility.

Second, although the studies reported here emphasize moral reasoning, children's newly acquired awareness of autonomous epistemic agency should also have measurable consequences for their moral actions. Specifically, in recognizing such autonomy, children should also be in a better position to understand the place of their own and others' will, or personal agency, in situations involving difficult choices or arduous courses of action. For such children, not only should it now be possible for them to generate more sophisticated cognitive strategies of self-control (for example, abstract nonconsummatory ideation; see Mischel, 1996), they should also achieve a richer appreciation for matters of personal commitment and moral obligation. In short, coming to a more active conception of mental life greatly expands children's moral horizons and, with them, the areas of sociocognitive development needing further study.

Third, and finally, whatever empirical success our research efforts may be seen to hold stems directly from our critique of the pervasive empiricist assumptions that currently dominate the theories-of-mind literature. These assumptions, as we have tried to make clear, ultimately lead to a view of human action and epistemic life that eschews the possibility of autonomous agency. Still further, the mechanistic form of agency that is left in its place does little to sustain our commonsense intuitions about moral life. As it stands, then, the theories-of-mind enterprise is poorly positioned to expand its scope into the moral domain. Until this is recognized and room is made for a broader conception of agency, attempts to bridge the two literatures will fall well short of our collective expectations.

References

Astington, J. W. *The Child's Discovery of the Mind.* Cambridge, Mass.: Harvard University Press, 1993.

Astington, J. W. "The Paradox of Intention: Assessing Children's Metarepresentational Understanding." In B. F. Malle, L. J. Moses, and D. A. Baldwin (eds.), *Intentions and Intentionality: Foundations of Social Cognition.* Cambridge, Mass.: MIT Press, 2001.

Astington, J. W., and Gopnik, A. "Developing Understanding of Desire and Intention." In A. Whiten (ed.), *Natural Theories of Mind: Evolution, Development, and Simulation of Everyday Mindreading.* Oxford: Blackwell, 1991.

Bandura, A. *Social Foundations of Thought and Action: A Social Cognitive Theory.* Upper Saddle River, N.J.: Prentice-Hall, 1986.

Bickhard, M. H. *Cognition, Convention, and Communication.* New York: Praeger, 1980.

Blasi, A. "The Self as Subject in the Study of Personality." In D. Ozer, J. M. Healy Jr., A. J. Stewart (vol. eds.), and R. Hogan (series ed.), *Perspectives in Personality: Self and Emotion.* London: Jessica Kingsley, 1991.

Blasi, A. "Moral Understanding and the Moral Personality: The Process of Moral Integration." In W. M. Kurtines and J. L. Gewirtz (eds.), *Moral Development: An Introduction.* Needham Heights, Mass.: Allyn & Bacon, 1995.

Bratman, M. E. *Intention, Plans, and Practical Reason.* Cambridge, Mass.: Harvard University Press, 1987.

Campbell, J. *Understanding John Dewey: Nature and Cooperative Intelligence.* Chicago: Open Court, 1995.

Carpendale, J. I., and Chandler, M. J. "On the Distinction Between False Belief Understanding and Subscribing to an Interpretive Theory of Mind." *Child Development,* 1996, 67, 1686–1706.

Chandler, M. J., and Boyes, M. "Social-Cognitive Development." In B. B. Wolman (ed.), *Handbook of Developmental Psychology.* Upper Saddle River, N.J.: Prentice Hall, 1982.

Chandler, M. J., Greenspan, S., and Barenboim, C. "Judgments of Intentionality in Response to Videotaped and Verbally Presented Moral Dilemmas: The Medium Is the Message." *Child Development,* 1973, 44, 315–320.

Chandler, M. J., and Lalonde, C. "Shifting from an Interpretive Theory of Mind: Five- to Seven-Year-Olds' Changing Conceptions of Mental Life." In A. J. Sameroff and M. M. Haith (eds.), *The Five to Seven Year Shift: The Age of Reason and Responsibility.* Chicago: University of Chicago Press, 1996.

Chandler, M. J., Lalonde, C., and Sokol, B. "Causes and Reasons: Rescuing Magical Thinking from the Jaws of Social Determinism." Paper presented at the Fifteenth Biennial Meeting of the International Society for the Study of Behavior and Development, Bern, Switzerland, July 1998.

Chandler, M. J., and Sokol, B. W. "Representation Once Removed: Children's Developing Conceptions of Representational Life." In I. Sigel (ed.), *Development of Mental Representation: Theories and Applications.* Mahwah, N.J.: Erlbaum, 1999.

Chandler, M. J., Sokol, B. W., and Hallett, D. "Moral Responsibility and the Interpretive Turn: Children's Changing Conceptions of Truth and Rightness." In B. F. Malle, L. J.

Moses, and D. A. Baldwin (eds.), *Intentions and Intentionality: Foundations of Social Cognition*. Cambridge, Mass.: MIT Press, 2001.

Churchland, P. M. *Matter and Consciousness*. Cambridge, Mass.: MIT Press, 1984.

Dewey, J. *Experience and Nature*. La Salle, Ill.: Open Court, 1989. (Originally published 1925.)

Duff, R. A. *Intention, Agency, and Criminal Liability: Philosophy of Action and the Criminal Law*. Oxford: Blackwell, 1990.

Fincham, F. D., and Roberts, C. "Intervening Causation and the Mitigation of Responsibility for Harm Doing." *Journal of Experimental Social Psychology*, 1985, 21, 178–194.

Frankfurt, H. G. *The Importance of What We Care About: Philosophical Essays*. Cambridge: Cambridge University Press, 1988.

Gopnik, A., and Wellman, H. M. "The Theory Theory." In L. A. Hirschfeld and S. A. Gelman (eds.), *Mapping the Mind: Domain Specificity in Cognition and Culture*. Cambridge: Cambridge University Press, 1994.

Hacker, P.M.S. *Wittgenstein: Mind and Will. An Analytical Commentary on the Philosophical Investigations*. Oxford: Blackwell, 1996.

Harré, R. *Personal Being: A Theory of Individual Psychology*. Oxford: Blackwell, 1982.

Harris, P. L., and others. "Young Children's Theory of Mind and Emotion." *Cognition and Emotion*, 1989, 3, 379–400.

Heider, F. *The Psychology of Interpersonal Relations*. New York: Wiley, 1958.

Hobson, R. P. *Autism and the Development of Mind*. Mahwah, N.J.: Erlbaum, 1993.

Joseph, R. M., and Tager-Flusberg, H. "Preschool Children's Understanding of the Desire and Knowledge Constraints on Intended Action." *British Journal of Developmental Psychology*, 1999, 17, 221–243.

Kenny, A. *Action, Emotion, and Will*. New York: Routledge and Kegan Paul, 1963.

Kim, J. *Philosophy of Mind*. Boulder, Colo.: Westview Press, 1996.

Lalonde, C. E. "Children's Understanding of the Interpretive Nature of the Mind." Unpublished doctoral dissertation, University of British Columbia, 1997.

Lalonde, C. E., and Chandler, M. J. "Children's Understanding of Interpretation." *New Ideas in Psychology*, 2002, 20, 163–198.

Malle, B. F. "How People Explain Behavior: A New Theoretical Framework." *Personality and Social Psychology Review*, 1999, 3, 23–48.

Malle, B. F., and Knobe, J. "The Distinction Between Desire and Intention: A Folk-Conceptual Analysis." In B. F. Malle, L. J. Moses, and D. A. Baldwin (eds.), *Intentions and Intentionality: Foundations of Social Cognition*. Cambridge, Mass.: MIT Press, 2001.

McNaughton, D. *Moral Vision: An Introduction to Ethics*. Oxford: Blackwell, 1988.

Meltzoff, A., and Gopnik, A. "The Role of Imitation in Understanding Persons and Developing a Theory of Mind." In S. Baron-Cohen, H. Tager-Flusberg, and D. J. Cohen (eds.), *Understanding Other Minds: Perspectives from Autism*. New York: Oxford University Press, 1993.

Meltzoff, A. N., Gopnik, A., and Repacholi, B. M. "Toddlers' Understanding of Intentions, Desires, and Emotions: Exploring the Dark Ages." In P. D. Zelazo, J. W. Astington, and D. R. Olson (eds.), *Developing Theories of Intention: Social Understanding and Self-Control*. Mahwah, N.J.: Erlbaum, 1999.

Mischel, W. "From Good Intentions to Willpower." In P. M. Gollwitzer and J. A. Bargh (eds.), *The Psychology of Action: Linking Cognition and Motivation to Behavior*. New York: Guilford Press, 1996.

Nelson, S. A. "Factors Influencing Young Children's Use of Motives and Outcomes as Moral Criteria." *Child Development*, 1980, 51, 823–829.

Overton, W. F. "Historical and Contemporary Perspectives on Developmental Theory and Research Strategies." In R. Downs, L. Liben, and D. Palermo (eds.), *Visions of Aesthetics, the Environment, and Development: The Legacy of Joachim Wohlwill*. Mahwah, N.J.: Erlbaum, 1991.

Perner, J. *Understanding the Representational Mind.* Cambridge, Mass.: MIT Press, 1991.

Piaget, J. *The Moral Judgment of the Child* (M. Gabain, trans.). New York: Free Press, 1965. (Originally published 1932.)

Pillow, B. H. "The Development of Children's Beliefs About the Mental World." *Merrill-Palmer Quarterly,* 1988, *34,* 1–32.

Pillow, B. H. "Two Trends in the Development of Conceptual Perspective Taking: An Elaboration of the Passive-Active Hypothesis." *International Journal of Behavioral Development,* 1995, *18,* 649–676.

Price, R. *Droodles.* New York: Simon & Schuster, 1953.

Reid, T. "Essays on the Active Powers of Man." In *The Works of Thomas Reid, D.D.* (6th ed., Vol. 2). Edinburgh: Maclachlan and Stewart, 1863. (Originally published 1788.)

Ross, S. D. *The Nature of Moral Responsibility.* Detroit, Mich.: Wayne State University, 1973.

Schult, C. A. "Intended Actions and Intentional States: Young Children's Understanding of the Causes of Human Actions." Unpublished doctoral dissertation, University of Michigan, 1996.

Searle, J. R. *Intentionality: An Essay in the Philosophy of Mind.* Cambridge: Cambridge University Press, 1983.

Skinner, B. F. "Answers for My Critics." In H. Wheeler (ed.), *Beyond the Punitive Society: Operation Conditioning: Social and Political Aspects.* New York: Freeman, 1973.

Sokol, B. W. "Intention, Interpretation, and Moral Responsibility: Children's Changing Beliefs About Truth and Rightness." Unpublished master's thesis, University of British Columbia, 1998.

Sokol, B. W., Jones, C. P., Paul, D., and Chandler, M. J. "Agency, Interpretation, and Responsibility: The Relationship Between Children's Moral Reasoning and an Interpretive Theory of Mind." Paper presented at the Association for Moral Education, University of Glasgow, U.K., July 2000.

Taylor, R. *Metaphysics.* Upper Saddle River, N.J.: Prentice Hall, 1963.

Taylor, R. *Action and Purpose.* Upper Saddle River, N.J.: Prentice Hall, 1966.

Velleman, J. D. "What Happens When Someone Acts?" In J. M. Fischer and M. Ravizza (eds.), *Perspectives on Moral Responsibility.* Ithaca, N.Y.: Cornell University Press, 1993.

Velleman, J. D. *The Possibility of Practical Reason.* Oxford: Clarendon Press, 2000.

Wellman, H., and Hickling, A. "The Mind's 'I': Children's Conception of the Mind as an Active Agent." *Child Development,* 1994, *65,* 1564–1580.

Wellman, H. M. *The Child's Theory of Mind.* Cambridge, Mass.: MIT Press, 1990.

White, P. A. *The Understanding of Causation and the Production of Action: From Infancy to Adulthood.* Mahwah, N.J.: Erlbaum, 1995.

Wimmer, H., and Perner, J. "Beliefs About Beliefs: Representation and Constraining Function of Wrong Beliefs in Young Children's Understanding of Deception." *Cognition,* 1983, *13,* 103–128.

BRYAN W. SOKOL is an assistant professor of psychology at Simon Fraser University.

MICHAEL J. CHANDLER is professor of psychology at the University of British Columbia.

CHRISTOPHER JONES is a doctoral student at Simon Fraser University.

3

The authors explore children's use of intention information in evaluating the moral quality of others' actions. They also address links among mental state understanding, motives-based moral reasoning, and children's own moral behavior.

The Role of Mental State Understanding in the Development of Moral Cognition and Moral Action

Jodie A. Baird, Janet Wilde Astington

A central topic within the theories-of-mind literature is when and how young children come to interpret actions in terms of underlying psychological motivations. The question is not simply, "When do children understand others' actions?" but rather, "When do children understand others' actions in the light of the actors' beliefs, desires, and intentions?" This focus on psychological states is similarly fundamental in the domain of moral judgment. As Kant (1959) remarked, "When moral worth is in question, it is not a matter of *actions* which one sees but of their *inner principles* which one does not see" (p. 23, emphasis added). Taking this notion as a starting point, the primary aim of our research program is to explore children's ability to consider mental states in evaluating the moral quality of others' actions. In particular, the work described here investigates children's ability to evaluate identical actions differently depending on the actors' motives.

A second question we aim to address is whether and how children's motives-based moral reasoning relates to the moral quality of their own behavior. It is commonly assumed that children's understanding of mental states has practical importance for their evolving social competence (Baird

---

This research was supported by a postdoctoral fellowship to the first author from the National Institute of Child Health and Human Development (#5 F32 HD08594–03). We are grateful to Jonathan Leef and Elif Gocek for their help with data collection and to Diego Fernandez-Duque and Bryan Sokol for helpful comments on an earlier draft of this chapter.

and Moses, 2001; Dunn, 1994; Flavell and Miller, 1998; Forguson and Gopnik, 1988; Leekam, 1993; Moore and Frye, 1991). Our research investigates this assumption, exploring the links among motives-based moral reasoning, mental state understanding, and moral behavior.

Motives-Based Moral Reasoning

Motive is one of two distinct aspects of intention that are central to the adult system of moral reasoning (Berndt and Berndt, 1975; Keasey, 1978; Malle, 1999). First, the intentionality of an act—that is, whether a behavior is intentional or accidental—influences how that act is evaluated. In most legal systems, for example, intentional acts of killing (murder) are judged more harshly than accidental acts of killing (manslaughter). Second, when evaluating actions performed intentionally, it is crucial to consider the actor's motive—the specific reason for acting. For example, a person who murders to save the lives of her children may be judged and punished differently from a person who murders to inherit a fortune.

The corpus of research on the development of moral reasoning has focused primarily on children's considerations of intentionality in evaluating behavior. Piaget (1965) conducted the first studies on this topic, devising stories in which two characters achieved a similar outcome either by accident or on purpose. For example, one story contrasted a boy who accidentally spilled a large amount of ink while trying to help his father with a boy who intentionally made a tiny inkblot. Children were asked to determine which boy was naughtier. Piaget reported that before age eight or nine, children's moral attributions focused primarily on the amount of damage caused by the action rather than on the intentionality of the action. In more recent years, however, this conclusion has been questioned due to methodological problems in Piaget's research. For example, Piaget confounded intentions and consequences; that is, the boy who accidentally spilled the ink did more damage than the boy who meant to spill the ink. Studies that correct for these kinds of problems have demonstrated earlier success. For example, when the amount of damage is held constant or when information about intentions is highlighted, children as young as age four or five can evaluate behavior on the basis of intentionality (Farnill, 1974; Karniol, 1978; Keasey, 1978; Nelson-Le Gall, 1985; Wellman, Larkey, and Somerville, 1979). However, children's evaluations of intentional versus unintentional behavior become increasingly differentiated with age (Buchanan and Thompson, 1973; Gutkin, 1972; Hebble, 1971; Imamoglu, 1975).

In contrast to the abundant literature on children's moral judgments of intentional versus unintentional behavior, few studies have investigated whether children recognize that even when two people intentionally perform identical behaviors, different evaluations may be justified depending on the actors' specific motives. In one such study (Nelson, 1980), three and seven year olds heard four different stories in which a boy purposely threw a ball toward a friend. All possible combinations of good and bad motives (to play catch with his friend; to hit his friend) and positive and negative outcomes (friend catches the ball; friend is hit by the ball) were presented. Following each story, children were asked to determine whether the boy who threw the ball was "good" or "bad." Nelson found that children of both ages judged the boy more favorably when he acted on a good motive rather than a bad motive, regardless of the outcome. However, research by Yuill (1984) suggests that outcomes outweigh motives in young children's moral evaluations. Three and five year olds in her study rated an actor with a good motive more favorably than an actor with a bad motive only when the value of the outcome matched the value of the motive. It was not until seven years of age that children in Yuill's study differentiated the actors on the basis of motives, independent of outcomes.

The findings from Nelson (1980) and Yuill (1984) suggest that between three and seven years of age, children recognize that identical actions may be evaluated differently depending on the actors' motives. However, the inclusion of outcome information in both of these studies makes it difficult to assess children's ability to consider motives alone in evaluating the moral quality of others' actions (Keasey, 1978). Moreover, although the story characters' actions were the same in the studies by Nelson (1980) and Yuill (1984), they were presented to children on different trials. A more stringent test of children's ability to evaluate identical actions differently necessitates the juxtaposition of two people performing identical actions in one and the same trial. Finally, Nelson (1980) and Yuill (1984) examined children's moral judgments in a single action context, ball throwing. A more thorough investigation of children's motives-based moral reasoning requires the use of varied action contexts.

Recent research on children's use of motives in interpreting behavior provides a fruitful model for assessing children's use of motives in evaluating behavior. In a series of studies by Baird and Moses (2001), four and five year olds heard stories in which two characters performed the same action (such as running) yet had different distal motives (for example, to be home for dinner versus to be healthy and strong). Children were asked to infer each character's proximal motive (for example, to get somewhere fast versus to get some exercise). Five year olds successfully attributed different proximal motives to the two characters, despite the fact that the characters' actions were identical. Four year olds, in contrast, tended to attribute the same proximal motive to both characters, even though they understood that the characters' distal motives differed.

We have now extended this methodology to address the question of whether children can evaluate identical actions differently depending on the actors' motives. Children who were ages four, five, and seven heard stories in which two characters performed the same action yet had markedly different motives. The key feature distinguishing the motives was their moral quality. In particular, one character had a good motive and the other character had a bad motive. For example, one story depicted two girls, Jessica and Susan, both of whom were turning on a hose. However, despite their identical actions, the girls' motives differed. Jessica's mother had planted some seeds in the backyard, and Jessica wanted to help take care of the garden ("good" motive), whereas Susan's brother had built a sand castle in the backyard, and Susan wanted the sand castle to collapse ("bad" motive).

It is important to note that the actions we selected, such as turning on a hose in this example or turning the music off in another story, are themselves neutral. None of the actions would typically be evaluated as "good" or "bad." Moreover, the stories did not include any information about the outcomes or consequences of the characters' actions. Thus, in order to evaluate the actions differently, children must consider the characters' motives; they could not simply defer to a canonical interpretation of the action or its consequence in making their moral judgments.

Children heard six different stories, each with a different action context. For each story, control questions were asked to ensure that children both recognized that the actions of the two characters were identical and remembered each character's specific desire. Of central interest was whether children would differentiate the characters' actions in terms of moral quality. We assessed children's moral judgments in two ways (for a similar methodology, see Helwig, Zelazo, and Wilson, 2001; Zelazo, Helwig, and Lau, 1996). First, we asked children to evaluate each character's action on a scale from "really good" to "really bad" (act evaluation measure). We then asked children to determine whether each character should "get in trouble" for performing the action (punishment measure). The following sections describe the method and results for each of these measures in turn.

Act Evaluation Measure. This measure assessed whether children could evaluate the actions of the two characters differently. For each character, children selected one of three colored faces to indicate whether the character's action was "good" (yellow smiling face), "bad" (red frowning face), or "not good or bad" (white neutral face). In particular, children were reminded of the character's action (for example, "Jessica is turning on the hose") and then were asked, "Is she doing a good thing, is she doing a bad thing, or is it not good or bad?" If children responded "good," they were asked to quantify their response (e.g., "How good? Just a little good, or really good?"). Children were similarly asked to quantify their response if they evaluated the action as "bad."

Children's evaluation of each character's action was coded numerically on a five-point scale, ranging from -2 ("really bad") to 2 ("really good"), with "not good or bad" coded as 0. Of central interest was whether children differentiated the two story characters in their act evaluations. Therefore, we calculated the difference between children's evaluation of the good character and their evaluation of the bad character. For example, if children rated the action of the "good" character as "really good" and the action of

Table 3.1. Mean Scores on the Moral Reasoning Task by Participant Group

Measure, Possible Range	Participant Group			
	Four Year Olds (N = 12)	Five Year Olds (N = 12)	Typically Developing Seven Year Olds (N = 11)	Behavior-Disordered Seven Year Olds (N = 7)
Act evaluation, −4 to 4	1.90 (1.46)	2.93 (.65)	2.78 (.59)	2.71 (1.38)
Punishment, −1 to 1	.52 (.37)	.77 (.17)	.84 (.12)	.77 (.34)

Note: Standard deviations are in parentheses.

the "bad" character as "a little bad," they would earn a difference score of 3 (2 minus −1). Difference scores ranged from −4 to 4. Positive scores indicated that children differentiated the characters appropriately in their evaluations, whereas a difference score of 0 indicated that children did not distinguish the characters in their evaluations. Children's scores were averaged across five of the stories. (A comparison of the six stories revealed that with respect to the punishment measure, one story generated more difficulty for children than any of the other stories. Hence, children's responses to this story were excluded. The pattern of findings remained the same whether or not the item was included.) Table 3.1 summarizes children's act evaluation scores by age (of current relevance are the first three columns; the fourth column describes a group of behavior-disordered children, discussed later in the chapter). A one-way analysis of variance (ANOVA) on these scores with age (four, five, and seven years old) as the between-subjects factor was significant, $F(2, 32) = 3.76$, $p < .05$. Post hoc comparisons using Fisher's least significant difference tests revealed that four year olds were significantly worse than both five year olds ($p < .02$) and seven year olds ($p < .05$) at differentiating the characters' actions in terms of moral quality. In contrast, five and seven year olds were equally skilled at assigning different moral evaluations to characters performing identical actions. Thus, children's ability to use motive information to differentially evaluate identical actions improved significantly between the ages of four and five, after which point it leveled off.

Punishment Measure. This measure assessed whether children would assign different amounts of punishment to the two story characters despite their identical actions. In particular, children were asked whether each character should be punished for performing the action (for example, "Should Jessica get in trouble for turning on the hose?"). If children stated "yes," they were asked to quantify their response (for example, "A little trouble, or a lot of trouble?").

Preliminary examination of children's punishment ratings indicated that they did not take full advantage of the three-point scale (0 = no trouble, 1 = a little trouble, 2 = a lot of trouble). Instead, when they assigned punishment, they tended to assign a lot (73 percent) rather than a little (27 percent) (binomial probability, $p < .0001$). Therefore, children's punishment ratings were coded on a two-point scale to indicate simply whether any punishment was assigned (0 = no trouble, 1 = a little or a lot of trouble). As with the act evaluation measure, of central interest was whether children differentiated the story characters in their assignments of punishment. Therefore, we calculated the difference between children's punishment of the bad character and their punishment of the good character. Difference scores ranged from -1 to 1. Children's scores were averaged across the five stories.

Table 3.1 summarizes children's punishment scores by age. A one-way ANOVA on these scores with age (four, five, and seven years old) as the between-subjects factor was significant, $F(2, 32) = 5.48, p < .01$. Post hoc comparisons using Fisher's least significant difference tests revealed that four year olds were significantly worse than both five year olds ($p < .02$) and seven year olds ($p < .005$) at differentiating the characters in terms of punishment. Five and seven year olds, however, were equally skilled at assigning different levels of punishment to characters performing identical actions. Thus, as with their performance on the act evaluation measure, children's ability to use motive information in their assignments of punishment improved significantly between the ages of four and five.

False-Belief Tasks. In addition to the motives-based moral reasoning task, we administered first-order false-belief tasks to four and five year olds as standard measures of their mental state understanding (Perner, Leekam, and Wimmer, 1987; Wimmer and Perner, 1983). These tasks required children to infer another person's belief when that belief conflicted with reality (for example, John thinks his toy is in the box but in fact it is in the basket).

Of interest was whether children's performance on the false-belief tasks correlated with their performance on the moral reasoning task, which also required mental state understanding. In fact, children's false-belief scores were significantly correlated with their scores on the act evaluation measure, $r(22) = .66, p < .005$ and the punishment measure, $r(22) = .62, p < .005$, even when controlling for the effects of age, $pr(21) = .59$ and $.55, p < .005$ and $.01$, respectively.

Thus, children's motives-based moral reasoning was positively correlated with their false-belief understanding. Importantly, this finding demonstrates a relation between children's theory of mind and the domain of moral judgment. Given the relevance of intention to the determination of moral worth, it is often assumed that children's mental state understanding would be related to their moral reasoning skills. Our work provides clear empirical evidence of that relation.

Summary. The aim of the research just described was to investigate children's ability to use information about motives to differentially evaluate identical actions. With respect to this aim, we found that five and seven year olds were more likely than four year olds both to evaluate and to punish identical actions differently on the basis of the actors' motives. It was not the case that four year olds were wholly incapable of using motive information to differentially evaluate identical actions, but they did not distinguish between the actions as strongly as did older children. These results both confirm and extend the findings of Baird and Moses (2001) demonstrating that relative to five year olds, four year olds have difficulty attributing different motives to characters who are performing identical actions.

Our findings also speak to those of Yuill (1984), who found that seven year olds could differentially evaluate identical actions on the basis of motives in any circumstance, whereas three and five year olds could do so only when the value of the outcome matched the value of the motive. The fact that five year olds in our study had little difficulty evaluating identical actions differently may have been due to the absence of outcome information. In a review of studies investigating children's evaluations of intentional versus accidental actions, Keasey (1978) noted that the mere presence of outcome information reduced children's ability to demonstrate their understanding of the accidental-intentional distinction, even when the outcomes of the accidental and intentional actions were identical. By eliminating outcome information in our stories, we were able to assess children's intrinsic ability to use information about motives to differentially evaluate identical actions, which may explain why we found success at younger ages than did Yuill (1984).

A second strength of our approach is that we assessed children's motives-based moral reasoning across a number of different action contexts (including turning on a hose and turning the music off, among others), as opposed to a single action context (throwing a ball; Nelson, 1980; Yuill, 1984). By varying the action context across stories, we are better positioned to generalize our findings. Overall, we did not find significant performance differences across stories, suggesting that children's ability to use motive information in their moral evaluations is independent from the actions they are evaluating, at least when the actions are neutral.

Links to Moral Behavior

The second goal of our research program is to investigate whether and how children's use of mental state information in evaluating others' behavior relates to the moral quality of children's own behavior. We employed two methods to investigate this link. First, we included in our research a group of seven year olds with aggression and other behavior disorders. Previous research by Dodge and colleagues suggests that relative to other children, aggressive and socially rejected children are less skilled at interpreting the intentions (that is, motives) of others (Dodge, 1980; Dodge and Frame, 1982; Dodge, Murphy, and Buchsbaum, 1984). By including such a group in our research, we could compare the motives-based moral reasoning skills of behavior-disordered children with those of typically developing children of the same age. Second, in addition to our laboratory measures of moral reasoning and mental state understanding, we obtained teacher reports of children's positive (for example, prosocial) and negative (for example, aggressive) classroom behavior. The inclusion of this teacher measure allowed us to examine relations between children's motives-based moral reasoning and their everyday social behavior.

Behavior-Disordered Children. To test for intact or impaired moral reasoning in children with behavior disorders, we included a group of seven year olds who were enrolled in a day treatment program at a psychiatric hospital for problems of aggression and social dysfunction. Of interest was whether these behavior-disordered children were as sophisticated in their moral judgments as typically developing children of the same age. In fact, the behavior-disordered seven year olds performed as well as the typically developing seven year olds on both the act evaluation measure and the punishment measure (see Table 3.1 for means). However, in contrast to the typically developing seven year olds, the behavior-disordered seven year olds performed no better than four year olds on either measure, $t(17) > 1.20$, ns. That is, while the moral-reasoning ability of behavior-disordered seven year olds was not statistically any worse than that of typically developing seven year olds, neither was it any better than that of four year olds.

In addition to the moral reasoning task, we administered second-order false-belief tasks (Homer and Astington, 2001; Perner and Wimmer, 1985; Sullivan, Zaitchik, and Tager-Flusberg, 1994) to both groups of seven year olds to test for intact or impaired mental state understanding among the behavior-disordered children. Similar to the first-order false-belief tasks, the second-order tasks require children to infer another person's belief when that belief conflicts with reality. However, whereas in the first-order task the person holds a mistaken belief about the state of the world, in the second-order task, the person holds a mistaken belief about another person's knowledge (for example, Mary thinks that Tom does not know she hid his crayon, but in fact he does know).

The behavior-disordered children performed significantly worse on the second-order false-belief tasks ($M = .57$ out of 2, $SD = .79$) than their typically developing age-mates ($M = 1.36$, $SD = .67$), $t(16) = 2.28$, $p < .05$, suggesting that relative to typically developing children, aggressive and socially dysfunctional children have difficulty understanding the mental states of others. Consistent with our findings, research by McKeough and colleagues suggests that aggressive children demonstrate less complexity in their mental state reasoning than do typically developing children (McKeough, Yates, and Marini, 1994). Moreover, numerous studies by Dodge and colleagues suggest that aggressive children are less skilled than typically developing children at interpreting the intentions (that is, mental states) of others (Dodge, 1980; Dodge and Frame, 1982).

As with the first-order false-belief tasks, we also investigated whether children's performance on the second-order false-belief tasks correlated with their performance on the moral reasoning task. Similar to the results with the first-order tasks, we found that children's scores on the second-order tasks were significantly correlated with their scores on the act evaluation measure, $r(16) = .53$, $p < .05$ (when controlling for the effects of age, $pr(15) = .46$, $p = .06$). Thus, across all groups of children, including those with behavioral aggression, motives-based moral reasoning was positively correlated with mental state understanding.

Teacher Report of Everyday Classroom Behavior. Our second method of investigating the relation between children's motives-based moral reasoning and the morality of their own behavior was to obtain teacher reports of children's everyday classroom behavior. In particular, our goal was to gather information regarding the frequency with which children engage in both negative and positive social behaviors. Therefore, the twenty-three-item teacher report consisted of four subscales: relational aggression (six items—for example, "tries to get others to dislike a peer"), overt aggression (six items—for example, "kicks or hits others"), prosocial behavior (five items—for example, "shares with others"), and peer competence (six items—for example, "seeks out other children to play with"). The relational aggression and overt aggression subscales were taken from the Preschool Social Behavior Scale—Teacher Form (Crick, Casas, and Mosher, 1997), and the prosocial behavior and peer competence subscales were taken from the Preschool Adjustment Questionnaire (Jewsuwan, Luster, and Kostelnik, 1993). Teachers indicated how well each item described the child they were rating using a three-point response scale corresponding to the frequency with which the child typically displayed the behavior (rarely, sometimes, frequently).

As expected, a positive correlation emerged between the prosocial behavior and peer competence subscales, as well as between the two aggression subscales. Negative correlations emerged between overt aggression and both prosocial behavior and peer competence. All of these correlations remained significant when controlling for age (see Table 3.2). Of central interest was whether teacher reports of children's everyday social behavior correlated with children's performance on tasks of social understanding (moral reasoning task and false-belief tasks). In this respect, two important findings emerged. First, in our sample of five year olds, children's performance on the moral reasoning task (act evaluation measure) was negatively correlated with teacher reports of overt aggression, $r(10) = -.78$, $p < .005$. This correlation remained significant when controlling for age, $pr(9) = -.78$, $p < .01$. Thus, five year olds who frequently displayed physical aggression toward their peers (as rated by their teachers) were less skilled at using information about motives to differentially evaluate identical actions. Similarly, Dunn, Cutting, and Demetriou (2000) found that four year olds characterized by a high level of conflict in their interactions with

Table 3.2. Correlations Among Teacher Report Subscales

Variables	Relational Aggression	Overt Aggression	Prosocial Behavior
Overt aggression	.48** (.45**)		
Prosocial behavior	−.11 (−.11)	−.36* (−.36*)	
Peer competence	−.19 (−.20)	−.35* (−.38*)	.64*** (.66***)

Note: Partial correlations controlling for age are shown in parentheses. N = 42. For correlations with relational aggression, N = 41.
*$p < .05$; **$p < .005$; ***$p < .0001$.

friends were less likely to justify moral judgments in reference to other people's feelings.

The second finding to emerge from the teacher report was a positive correlation between children's second-order false-belief understanding and their teachers' ratings of prosocial behavior and peer competence, $r(16) = .67$ and $.49$, $p < .005$ and $.05$, respectively. These correlations remained strong when controlling for age: prosocial behavior: $pr(15) = .62$, $p < .01$; peer competence: $pr(15) = .41$, $p < .10$. In other words, children who frequently demonstrated positive social behaviors, such as cooperating with peers and offering to help, were more skilled at inferring the mental states of others. This finding is consistent with those of other studies demonstrating that false-belief understanding is a significant predictor of both teacher ratings of children's positive social skills (Watson, Nixon, Wilson, and Capage, 1999) and peer ratings of children's popularity (Angelopoulos and Moore, 2000; Dockett, 1997). However, whereas previous studies included only first-order false-belief tasks, our research demonstrates a link between second-order false-belief understanding and real-world social behavior. The ability to infer mental states when the contents of those mental states include the thoughts and beliefs of other people may be particularly important for children's success in the social world.

Motives, Morals, and Behavior

The findings from our research reveal that five and seven year olds can use information about people's motives to make moral distinctions between identical actions. The findings also demonstrate that this ability is positively related to children's false-belief understanding and negatively related to their behavioral aggression. This work therefore helps to bridge two gaps that are a focus of current interest in the field of social-cognitive development. First, our project is one of several recent attempts (this volume included) to link moral reasoning and theory-of-mind research (Chandler, Sokol, and Hallett, 2001; Dunn, Cutting, and Demetriou, 2000; Hughes and

Dunn, 2000; Wainryb and Ford, 1998); here we demonstrate a positive relation between moral reasoning ability and false-belief task performance. Second, our research links children's cognitive abilities and their real-world social behavior in the areas of both moral reasoning and social understanding. We show that motives-based moral reasoning is negatively related to aggressive behavior, and second-order false-belief understanding is positively related to prosocial behavior and peer competence. Of course, our findings do not speak to the causal direction of these relations. Studies that incorporate longitudinal or training methodologies are needed to determine the precise nature of the relations among moral reasoning, social understanding, and real-world behavior.

Moral development research has a long history of concern with children's reasoning about and judgments of people's actions, based on consideration of their mental states. Relatedly, although somewhat separately, over the past two decades, theory-of-mind researchers have investigated how children reason about beliefs and intentions in interpreting human action, with recent attention to individual differences in this development and to the social origins and implications of theory of mind. Thus, there are signs (the research reported here being one of these) that work in moral development and theory of mind is becoming more closely linked, which will be of benefit to both areas.

References

Angelopoulos, M., and Moore, C. "Theory of Mind and Social Behavior—The Child's Eye View." Unpublished manuscript, Dalhousie University, 2000.

Baird, J. A., and Moses, L. J. "Do Preschoolers Appreciate That Identical Actions May Be Motivated by Different Intentions?" *Journal of Cognition and Development,* 2001, 2, 413–448.

Berndt, T. J., and Berndt, E. G. "Children's Use of Motives and Intentionality in Person Perception and Moral Judgment." *Child Development,* 1975, 46, 904–912.

Buchanan, J. P., and Thompson, S. K. "A Quantitative Methodology to Examine the Development of Moral Judgment." *Child Development,* 1973, 44, 186–189.

Chandler, M. J., Sokol, B. W., and Hallett, D. "Moral Responsibility and the Interpretive Turn: Children's Changing Conceptions of Truth and Rightness." In B. F. Malle, L. J. Moses, and D. A. Baldwin (eds.), *Intentions and Intentionality: Foundations of Social Cognition.* Cambridge, Mass.: MIT Press, 2001.

Crick, N. R., Casas, J. F., and Mosher, M. "Relational and Overt Aggression in Preschool." *Developmental Psychology,* 1997, 33, 579–588.

Dockett, S. "Young Children's Peer Popularity and Theories of Mind." Poster presented at the biennial meeting of the Society for Research in Child Development, Washington, D.C., Apr. 1997.

Dodge, K. A. "Social Cognition and Children's Aggressive Behavior." *Child Development,* 1980, 51, 162–170.

Dodge, K. A., and Frame, C. L. "Social Cognitive Biases and Deficits in Aggressive Boys." *Child Development,* 1982, 53, 620–635.

Dodge, K. A., Murphy, R. R., and Buchsbaum, K. "The Assessment of Intention-Cue Detection Skills in Children: Implications for Developmental Psychopathology." *Child Development,* 1984, 55, 163–173.

Dunn, J. "Changing Minds and Changing Relationships." In C. Lewis and P. Mitchell (eds.), *Children's Early Understanding of Mind: Origins and Development*. Mahwah, N.J.: Erlbaum, 1994.

Dunn, J., Cutting, A. L., and Demetriou, H. "Moral Sensibility, Understanding Others, and Children's Friendship Interactions in the Preschool Period." *British Journal of Developmental Psychology*, 2000, 18, 159–177.

Farnill, D. "The Effects of Social-Judgment Set on Children's Use of Intent Information." *Journal of Personality*, 1974, 42, 276–289.

Flavell, J. H., and Miller, P. H. "Social Cognition." In W. Damon (series ed.), D. Kuhn and R. Siegler (vol. eds.), *Handbook of Child Psychology*, Vol. 2: *Cognition, Perception, and Language*. (5th ed.) New York: Wiley, 1998.

Forguson, L., and Gopnik, A. "The Ontogeny of Common Sense." In J. W. Astington, P. L. Harris, and D. R. Olson (eds.), *Developing Theories of Mind*. Cambridge: Cambridge University Press, 1988.

Gutkin, D. C. "The Effect of Systematic Story Changes on Intentionality in Children's Moral Judgments." *Child Development*, 1972, 43, 187–195.

Hebble, P. W. "The Development of Elementary School Children's Judgment of Intent." *Child Development*, 1971, 42, 1203–1215.

Helwig, C. C., Zelazo, P. D., and Wilson, M. "Children's Judgments of Psychological Harm in Normal and Noncanonical Situations." *Child Development*, 2001, 72, 66–81.

Homer, B. D., and Astington, J. W. "Children's Representation of Second Order Beliefs in Self and Other." Unpublished manuscript, New York University, 2001.

Hughes, C., and Dunn, J. "Hedonism or Empathy? Hard-to-Manage Children's Moral Awareness and Links with Cognitive and Maternal Characteristics." *British Journal of Developmental Psychology*, 2000, 18, 227–245.

Imamoglu, E. O. "Children's Awareness and Usage of Intention Cues." *Child Development*, 1975, 46, 39–45.

Jewsuwan, R., Luster, T., and Kostelnik, M. "The Relation Between Parents' Perceptions of Temperament and Children's Adjustment to Preschool." *Early Childhood Research Quarterly*, 1993, 8, 33–51.

Kant, I. *Foundations of the Metaphysics of Morals* (L. W. Beck, trans.). New York: Macmillan, 1959. (Originally published 1785.)

Karniol, R. "Children's Use of Intention Cues in Evaluating Behavior." *Psychological Bulletin*, 1978, 85, 76–85.

Keasey, C. B. "Children's Developing Awareness and Usage of Intentionality and Motives." In C. B. Keasey (ed.), *Nebraska Symposium on Motivation*. Lincoln: University of Nebraska Press, 1978.

Leekam, S. "Children's Understanding of Mind." In M. Bennett (ed.), *The Child as Psychologist*. New York: Harvester Wheatsheaf, 1993.

Malle, B. F. "How People Explain Behavior: A New Theoretical Framework." *Personality and Social Psychology Review*, 1999, 3, 23–48.

McKeough, A., Yates, T., and Marini, A. "Intentional Reasoning: A Developmental Study of Behaviorally Aggressive and Normal Boys." *Development and Psychopathology*, 1994, 6, 285–304.

Moore, C., and Frye, D. "The Acquisition and Utility of Theories of Mind." In D. Frye and C. Moore (eds.), *Children's Theories of Mind: Mental States and Social Understanding*. Mahwah, N.J.: Erlbaum, 1991.

Nelson, S. A. "Factors Influencing Young Children's Use of Motives and Outcomes as Moral Criteria." *Child Development*, 1980, 51, 823–829.

Nelson-Le Gall, S. A. "Motive-Outcome Matching and Outcome Foreseeability: Effects on Attribution of Intentionality and Moral Judgments." *Developmental Psychology*, 1985, 21, 332–337.

Perner, J., Leekam, S. R., and Wimmer, H. "Three Year Olds' Difficulty with False Belief:

The Case for a Conceptual Deficit." *British Journal of Developmental Psychology*, 1987, 5, 125–137.

Perner, J., and Wimmer, H. "'John Thinks That Mary Thinks That. . . .': Attribution of Second-Order Beliefs by Five- to Ten-Year-Old Children." *Journal of Experimental Child Psychology*, 1985, 39, 437–471.

Piaget, J. *The Moral Judgment of the Child* (M. Gabain, trans.). New York: Free Press, 1965. (Originally published 1932.)

Sullivan, K., Zaitchik, D., and Tager-Flusberg, H. "Preschoolers Can Attribute Second-Order Beliefs." *Developmental Psychology*, 1994, 30, 395–402.

Wainryb, C., and Ford, S. "Young Children's Evaluations of Acts Based on Beliefs Different from Their Own." *Merrill-Palmer Quarterly*, 1998, 44, 484–503.

Watson, A. C., Nixon, C. L., Wilson, A., and Capage, L. "Social Interaction Skills and Theory of Mind in Young Children." *Developmental Psychology*, 1999, 35, 386–391.

Wellman, H. M., Larkey, C., and Somerville, S. C. "The Early Development of Moral Criteria." *Child Development*, 1979, 50, 869–873.

Wimmer, H., and Perner, J. "Beliefs About Beliefs: Representation and Constraining Function of Wrong Beliefs in Young Children's Understanding of Deception." *Cognition*, 1983, 13, 103–128.

Yuill, N. "Young Children's Coordination of Motive and Outcome in Judgements of Satisfaction and Morality." *British Journal of Developmental Psychology*, 1984, 2, 73–81.

Zelazo, P. D., Helwig, C. C., and Lau, A. "Intention, Act, and Outcome in Behavioral Prediction and Moral Judgment." *Child Development*, 1996, 67, 2478–2492.

JODIE A. BAIRD is a postdoctoral fellow in the Department of Human Development and Applied Psychology at the Ontario Institute for Studies in Education of the University of Toronto.

JANET WILDE ASTINGTON is professor and chair of the Department of Human Development and Applied Psychology at the Ontario Institute for Studies in Education of the University of Toronto.

4

Prosocial behavior requires both conceptual and motivational components. A full account of the development of prosocial behavior requires attention to the acquisition of both theory of mind and the tendency to organize action toward the interests of others and the future self.

Altruism, Prudence, and Theory of Mind in Preschoolers

Chris Moore, Shannon Macgillivray

The work reported in this chapter arose from two complementary lines of thinking. One was a consideration of the psychological mechanisms involved in organizing behavior that is not in the best immediate interests of the actor but rather is in the interests of someone else—in short, altruism. Clearly this issue is fundamentally about moral action. However, our thinking on the topic led us in a different direction from traditional work on the development of moral reasoning, which is primarily about the kinds of rules actors use to justify moral action (see Chapter Five, this volume). Instead, we considered how action could be motivated by interests or goals that were not the actor's own immediate ones. Goals or interests that are not an actor's own immediate ones include those that are attributable to another person or to the self in the future. We refer to these collectively as noncurrent goals or interests. In drawing the distinction between immediate and noncurrent interests and goals, we were led also to consider the connection between altruism and prudence. By prudence, we mean action that is designed to bring about some future desired goal of the self at the expense of some immediate goal. Typical examples drawn from everyday life are dieting, training for a sporting event, and saving money.

The work reported in this chapter was supported by a grant from the Social Sciences and Humanities Research Council of Canada to the first author. We are grateful to Sandra Bosacki, Karen Lemmon, Shana Nichols, Carol Thompson, and Katie Walker for their assistance on the studies and to Jodie Baird and Bryan Sokol for valuable comments on an earlier draft. Chris Moore thanks John Barresi for many discussions on the theoretical issues. This work would not have been possible without the dedication of our participant families, to whom we are especially grateful.

The relation between altruism and prudence has a venerable intellectual history, being a topic of some interest to writers such as John Locke and William Hazlitt (see Martin and Barresi, 1995). In their time, the issue was how a person could be naturally interested in the concerns of another person or the self at another time. A variety of solutions were proposed, but the one from Hazlitt has a remarkably modern sense to it: "The imagination, by means of which alone I can anticipate future objects, or be interested in them, must carry me out of myself into the feelings of others by one and the same process by which I am thrown forward as it were into my future being, and interested in it" (Hazlitt, 1969, p. 3).

The point that Hazlitt was making here is that there is a fundamental similarity between altruism and prudence: in both cases, the actor must imagine and empathize with a noncurrent state of affairs—the other person's in the case of altruism and one's own future in the case of prudence. As we shall see, where Hazlitt saw one and the same process, we identify two. Nevertheless, his ideas can be seen as a starting point for the work we describe here.

Altruism and prudence may be seen as two pillars of organized social behavior. Altruism is the organization of action with respect to others' goals. Prudence is the organization of action with respect to one's own future goals. This line of thinking about the nature of altruism and prudence led naturally to a second line of thinking, which was the idea that the function of theory of mind is to organize complex social behavior. From the beginning of the nearly twenty-five-year modern history of the notion of theory of mind, there has been the assumption that the ability to explain and predict behavior by attributing mental states to agents is functional in the organization of social behavior (Moore and Frye, 1991). In simple terms, it has been assumed that successful functioning in large social groups involves complexities of information handling that are to some extent simplified by postulating mental states governing behavior. Surprisingly little work, however, has directly addressed the relation between theory of mind and the organization of social behavior. Certainly there is a substantial literature on deception because of its obvious connection to false-belief understanding (Ruffman, Olson, Ash, and Keenan, 1993; Russell, Mauthner, Sharpe, and Tidswell, 1991). More recently, a number of researchers have turned to the investigation of relations between theory of mind and both prosocial and antisocial behavior (Hughes, White, Sharpen, and Dunn, 2000; Jenkins and Astington, 2000; Slomkowski and Dunn, 1996). But a general consideration of the link between theory of mind and organized social behavior has largely been neglected (but see Chapter Three, this volume).

In what follows, we briefly introduce the relevant issues from the theory-of-mind literature before going on to consider the connection between theory of mind, altruism, and prudence. We end by providing some recent evidence from our empirical program on this connection.

Theory of Mind

By *theory of mind,* we mean a conceptual system involving mental state categories, such as beliefs, desires, and intentions. These categories provide the conceptual means to explain and predict the behavior of agents, including both others and the self. Thus, we might say that John *intends* to go to the mall because he *thinks* Mary will be there and he *wants* to see her. Or, I sent my dad the CD because I *thought* he would *like* it. This kind of conceptual system develops during the preschool years and is clearly evident by five years of age (see Astington, Harris, and Olson, 1988).

The literature devoted to theory of mind is now so voluminous that a single chapter cannot do it justice. Here we pick out two points that are relevant to our immediate concern: how theory of mind may be related to prudence and altruism. The first point is that intrinsic to theory of mind is the notion that mental states vary across different agents or within the same agent at different times. As has been pointed out from the earliest days of theory-of-mind research, the key categories of theory of mind, such as belief, desire, and intention, presuppose diversity in the content of the mental states. Any representational mental state may differ from reality and may differ across individuals and within the same individual across time (Forguson and Gopnik, 1988). The most commonly used versions of theory-of-mind tasks—false belief and representational change—trade on this aspect of the conceptual system. False-belief tasks ask the child to predict what another person will think based on misleading exposure to some state of affairs in the world. Representational change tasks ask the child to report his or her own previous beliefs about the world based on similar misleading exposure. In both cases, a conflict between the content of the current belief and that to be reported is set up. To succeed in each case, the child must be aware of the conflict or diversity between the current (or true) state of affairs and the state of affairs as represented in the mind following exposure to misleading information. Results from numerous studies (Gopnik and Astington, 1988; Moore, Pure, and Furrow, 1990) have shown that at about four years of age, children start to be able to succeed in these kinds of tasks, thereby giving evidence that they understand that mental states may diverge across persons and across time.

The second point is that a theory of mind is equally applicable to self and others. This is perhaps most easily demonstrated by the fact that the subject of mental state propositions can be in either the first person or the second or third person. As a number of authors have pointed out (Barresi and Moore, 1996; Meltzoff and Gopnik, 1993; Moore and Barresi, 1993), this self-evident aspect of theory of mind actually conceals the nub of a profound developmental problem. Because the information available to any individual about his or her own mental states and those of others is qualitatively different (for example, we never have direct access to other people's mental content), there has to be some mechanism whereby those qualitatively different sources of information can be conceptualized in the same form. Various suggestions for this mechanism have been proposed (Barresi and Moore, 1996; Meltzoff and Gopnik, 1993), and we will not delve further into them here. For present purposes, it is important to note the parallelism between self and other in theory of mind.

The two issues identified here are not independent and are bound together by the fact that both depend on the operation of the imagination (Harris, 2000). It is the imagination that makes possible the representation of states of affairs and states of mind that are different from those currently experienced. Thus, representing diversity requires the operation of the imagination. It is the imagination that allows the individual to contemplate states of affairs that are different from those currently experienced, either because they belong to some other person or because they belong to the self at another time. Thus, it is the imagination that allows the individual to range cognitively across persons and across time.

How to Be Interested in Noncurrent Mental States

We now return to the parallel between prudence and altruism. How is it possible for action to be guided by the interests or concerns of another person or of the self at some future time? Even a cursory analysis suggests that a variety of psychological processes must be involved. First, the actor must be able to represent those noncurrent concerns, including the concerns of others and the concerns of self in the future. The simple idea is that the ability to imagine noncurrent mental states of self or other as distinct from current experience will allow the actor to implement behavior designed to bring about or prevent those future circumstances. Certainly, it would seem necessary that if the individual is going to act in the interests of another person, at least in those cases where the interests are not transparent in the other's behavior, then he or she must be able to represent those interests. To us, it seemed that this mapped closely onto theory of mind. In that sense, theory of mind must be a component of behavior designed to facilitate others' achievements. Similarly, to make a prudent choice, the individual should be able to represent the future circumstances of the self and compare those to the current circumstances.

However, representing the diversity of mental states of self and other cannot be enough. Given that in any social situation, both cooperation and competition are potential tactics, it must be the case that accompanying the representation of the noncurrent interests, there is a desire to act in their favor. If not, then the actor would automatically implement the action that was in the best immediate interests of himself or herself. In short, the individual must be able not only to represent the mental states of others and the future self but also to care about them. There must be a way in which the imagined state of affairs can achieve sufficient motivational power for it to override the motives provided by the current state of affairs.

We suggest that the natural tendency to empathize or "feel into" imagined states of affairs provides the necessary motivational power. Just as the mental states of others that are evident in their behavior, such as emotions, may lead to an empathic response, so the mental states of others that are imagined may similarly produce empathy for those states. Importantly, we claim that the imagined mental states of self in the future may also produce empathy. In short, imagining the noncurrent mental states of anyone, whether self or other, may produce an empathic reaction, and it is this reaction that guides behavior.

It is tempting to speculate on the factors that may influence such caring. It is likely, for example, that, other things being equal, perception of another's emotional state engenders a more intense empathic reaction than the imagination of that state. It may also be the case that, other things being equal, empathy for one's own future is a more powerful motivator than empathy for the imagined future circumstances of others. However, many other factors will moderate such comparisons. Indeed it is likely that more often than not, the other-things-being-equal clause does not hold, and empathy for another person's future circumstances can outweigh even one's own immediate motives.

This simple distinction between the representational and the motivational components of action organized toward noncurrent interests masks considerable complexity, and we do not claim to have identified all the psychological processes that are involved. For example, it is presumably the case that executive functions such as inhibitory control, attentional flexibility, and working memory play a part in allowing the actor to implement action organized toward imagined interests. It may also be that some ability to represent time's arrow, at least in the sense that the present is causally connected to the future, may be required (see Moore and Lemmon, 2001; Povinelli, 1995). These are important considerations, but to pursue them further here will distract us from our main purpose, which is to illustrate empirically the distinction between the representational and motivational components raised above.

Empirical Approaches

For our investigation into altruism and prudence, we have used a modification of the delay-of-gratification procedure. The traditional delay of gratification procedure presents children with an opportunity to take a small reward or, by resisting the impulse to take the small reward, to receive a larger reward. In our terms, delay of gratification reflects prudence. Mischel and colleagues have investigated a number of the parameters associated with delay of gratification, including age, length of delay, and effective strategies for delay (see Mischel, 1974). We changed the traditional procedure to a trial-based format and at the same time introduced choices that involved prosocial sharing options or, in our terms, altruism. In an initial study (Thompson, Barresi, and Moore, 1997), we sought to explore any changes in performance in our task that were associated with age, as well as to examine the relation between prudence and altruism. We presented three to five year olds with a series of two alternative choices for which the rewards were stickers. Along with a delay-of-gratification choice for which children could choose between one sticker immediately or two stickers later, children were presented with a variety of choices involving sharing. In two of these choice types, there was no delay. To assess sharing without cost, children were asked to choose between one sticker for self or one sticker each for both self and another person (a teenage confederate acting as a play partner). To assess sharing with cost, children were asked to choose between two stickers for self or one sticker each for self and partner. In a third sharing choice type, children were given a choice between one sticker for self now or one sticker for self and partner later. This third choice involved the same quantities as the sharing-without-cost choice, but the delay imposed for the sharing option meant that there was now a cost to sharing, albeit not a material one.

The results showed clear developmental effects for the choice types involving a delayed option, with three year olds tending to opt for the immediate rewards and five year olds opting to delay. For the choice types involving sharing without delay, there were no developmental effects. Three year olds were as likely as five year olds to opt to share with the play partner. While the tendency to share was lower in the case where there was a cost to sharing, there was still no effect of age. In addition to the developmental effects, there was also a significant association between the two trial types involving a delay. Children who tended to choose to share the stickers in the future also tended to delay their own gratification.

This initial study established the developmental period of interest for altruism and prudence in our sticker choice task. Perhaps not surprisingly, the critical developmental effects appeared at about four years of age, exactly the age when performance in standard theory-of-mind tasks improves. To explore this association empirically, in a follow-up experiment (Moore, Barresi, and Thompson, 1998) we presented three and four year olds with similar choice tasks and with theory-of-mind tasks (misleading contents version of the false-belief task and a conflicting-desire task). The results showed that for the four year olds, theory-of-mind performance was significantly correlated with the tendency to share in delay situations. That is, children who did well on theory-of-mind tasks tended to choose to share stickers with another even if it meant not being able to have the sticker now. These results were the first to indicate that theory of mind may be related to giving up one's own immediate gratification when that gratification conflicts with another's future interests.

These experiments were promising in showing that altruism and prudence did show changes from three to five years and that there was some evidence of a relation between theory of mind and future-oriented altruism.

However, there were clear limitations on the inferences possible from these initial experiments. Most obviously, there were no control variables apart from age. In addition, we were concerned about the nature of the variability observed in the sticker choice task. In fact, the distinction between the conceptual and motivational components of prudence and altruism requires us to take notice of two potential sources of variability in children's behavior. Much of the research on theory of mind has focused on developmental variability in the representation of diversity in mental states, and, as is well known, the period from three to five years has been identified as a time of significant developmental change. However, all normally developing children relatively quickly attain the same level of conceptual ability. In short, variability in theory of mind seen during the period from three to five years is largely attributable to developmental differences. Such may not be the case for the variability in the motivational component of social behavior. Indeed, it is likely that there are individual differences in the tendency to care about others or about one's own future that are relatively stable across age. So even if there is developmental variability in performance on these tasks around four years of age, it is likely that there is residual individual difference variation even after development is essentially complete.

These concerns led us to undertake a larger-scale longitudinal study of these tasks over the critical period of developmental transition. The rationale was that a longitudinal study would allow us to examine individual consistency over time as well as individual development. In the longitudinal study of about fifty-eight preschoolers, we tested children at three age points, six months apart, from about three and a half to about four and a half years. Children were brought to the laboratory at each age and given a battery of individual tasks. Not all children completed all tasks. At each age, they were tested on the sticker choice task using three trials of each of three choice types:

- Two for self now, one for each now
- Two for self now, one for each later
- One for self now, two for self later

Note that both sharing choice types in this study involved a cost to the self in sharing. In this way, the task is structured so that each choice type presents the child with a potential conflict between the interests of self and other or between the present and the future. Rewards were again small stickers. Those stickers that were taken immediately were placed into a sticker book by the child. Those that were saved were placed in an envelope for later. For the sharing choice types, the potential recipient was a research assistant who had played with the child during the visit in advance of the actual testing session. One point was allocated to the child each time he or she chose to share or to delay, yielding a possible score of 0 to 3 for each trial type.

Table 4.1. Means and Standard Deviations of the Measures Taken in the Longitudinal Study

	Three and a Half Years (N = 57)	Four Years (N = 53)	Four and a Half Years (N = 51)
Two for self now, one for each now	1.44 (1.07)	1.70 (1.17)	2.04 (1.00)
Two for self now, one for each later	1.19 (0.99)	1.17 (1.05)	1.73 (1.22)
One for self now, two for self later	1.56 (1.07)	1.30 (1.20)	1.49 (1.14)
Theory of mind		2.68 (1.49)	

Note: Standard deviations are in parentheses.

During the visit at four years, the testing session also included five different theory-of-mind tasks. These tasks were modeled on standard protocols (Gopnik and Astington, 1988; Moore, Pure, and Furrow, 1990) and assessed false belief using both misleading objects and displaced objects as well as representational change using misleading objects. Performance on each task was scored as correct or incorrect, and scores were summed across the five tasks to yield an aggregate theory-of-mind score ranging from 0 to 5. To control for general verbal intelligence, we assessed the children using the Peabody Picture Vocabulary Test—III (PPVT-III, Dunn and Dunn, 1997) at age three and a half and four and a half.

Descriptive statistics for the sticker choice tasks and for the theory-of-mind measure are shown in Table 4.1. Performance on both sharing choice types increased significantly with age from three and a half to four and a half, but at each age, sharing in the present was a more favored option than delayed sharing. However, performance on the prudence choice type did not change across the year of the study. Performance on the theory-of-mind measure showed variability typical of that normally found at four years of age.

A number of correlational analyses were performed. First, we examined consistency in performance on the sticker choice tasks across age. These results showed that whereas there was good consistency in all three choice types from four to four and a half years (r ranged from .337 to .495, $p < .01$), performance at three and a half years did not correlate significantly with performance on the same task at the two older ages. These results suggest that at least by four years of age, children are relatively consistent in how they make their choices in the three choice types.

Second, we examined correlations among the choice types at each age (see Table 4.2). Here we found different patterns of correlation at each age. At three and a half years, the two sharing choice types were significantly

Table 4.2. Zero-Order Correlations Among Three Trial Types at Ages Three and a Half, Four, and Four and a Half

	Two for Self Now, One for Each Now	Two for Self Now, One for Each Later	One for Self Now, Two for Self Later
Age three and a half (N = 57)			
Two for self now, one for each now	1.000	.492*	−.081
Two for self now, one for each later		1.000	−.070
One for self now, two for self later			1.000
Age four (N = 53)			
Two for self now, one for each now	1.000	.540*	.377*
Two for self now, one for each later		1.000	.635*
One for self now, two for self later			1.000
Age four and a half (N = 51)			
Two for self now, one for each now	1.000	.376*	−.017
Two for self now, one for each later		1.000	.519*
One for self now, two for self later			1.000

Note: *$p < .05$.

correlated, indicating that at least performance was not random at this age and that children were consistent in their sharing across the two types of sharing opportunity. However, there was no relation between the sharing choice types and prudence. Our feeling here is that the children at this age simply did not understand the prudence choice type well enough to answer reliably. Indeed, many of them tended to choose two stickers in the prudence choice but then appeared disappointed when they did not get the stickers immediately. In short, despite very explicit instructions, they appeared not to be able to treat this task as a choice between now and later. Nevertheless, there was evidence of individual differences in sharing.

By four years, a consistent pattern of correlations across choice tasks had arisen. All three of the tasks were significantly correlated with each other. These correlations remained significant even after the PPVT-III score was controlled in partial correlations. One inference from this pattern is that there was some common psychological capacity underlying performance in all three trial types. This inference is bolstered by the finding that at this age, performance on the delayed-sharing choice was significantly correlated with theory-of-mind score ($r = .331$; $p < .05$), as we had found in our earlier study (Moore, Barresi, and Thompson, 1998). Interestingly, the significance of the correlation between theory of mind and delayed sharing did not survive controlling for PPVT score. In short, it appears that there is developmental variability in sticker choice performance and that this variability is related to mental state understanding, although whether this relation is mediated by general verbal ability is an open question.

Finally, at four and a half years, a different pattern of correlations among the sticker choice tasks emerged. Now the two choices involving sharing were significantly correlated, as were the two choices involving delay, but there was no relation between simple sharing and simple delay of gratification. Furthermore, there were no relations with theory of mind or with PPVT score. Our interpretation of these results is that once the critical transition period for understanding conflicting mental states at about four years is over, there still remains significant residual individual variability in the willingness to share with others and in the willingness to delay gratification. This finding is consistent with the idea that the motivational components of action organization are separable from the representational component. It is possible, although by no means demonstrated, that the individual variability in the motivational component remains relatively stable from this point on.

If the latter interpretation is valid, then two obvious lines of research are opened up. First, it will be of considerable interest to explore the factors that may be related to the individual variability in sharing or prudence. We have started to explore the possibility that this variability may be related to aspects of the children's relationships (Moore and Symons, forthcoming). In particular, prudence appears to be quite strongly related to security of attachment. Second, the longer-term stability of these patterns and their correlates in children's social functioning will be of significant interest (Mischel, Shoda, and Rodriguez, 1990; Shoda, Mischel, and Peake, 1989).

Conclusion

In sum, children's ability to act in favor of the interests of another person and of themselves in the future develops around age four in parallel with their developing understanding of the diversity of mental states. However, there is reason to doubt on both theoretical and empirical grounds that the organization of social behavior with respect to noncurrent interests or goals is tightly tied to theory-of-mind development. For a child to act in favor of a person's noncurrent interests, he or she must be able not only to represent those goals but also to care about them. Our results suggest that the latter component of the organization of social behavior likely shows individual differences throughout development that are independent of the more cognitive aspects of theory of mind.

References

Astington, J. W., Harris, P. L., and Olson, D. R. (eds.). *Developing Theories of Mind.* Cambridge: Cambridge University Press, 1988.

Barresi, J., and Moore, C. "Intentional Relations and Social Understanding." *Behavioral and Brain Sciences,* 1996, *19,* 107–122.

Dunn, L., and Dunn, L. *Peabody Picture Vocabulary Test.* (3rd ed.) Circle Pines, Minn.: American Guidance Service, 1997.

Forguson, L., and Gopnik, A. "The Ontogeny of Commonsense." In J. W. Astington, P. L. Harris, and D. R. Olson (eds.), *Developing Theories of Mind.* Cambridge: Cambridge University Press, 1988.

Gopnik, A., and Astington, J. W. "Children's Understanding of Representational Change and Its Relation to the Understanding of False Belief and the Appearance-Reality Distinction." *Child Development,* 1988, *59,* 26–37.

Harris, P. L. *The Work of the Imagination.* Oxford: Blackwell, 2000.

Hazlitt, W. *An Essay on the Principles of Human Action and Some Remarks on the Systems of Hartley and Helvetius.* Gainesville, Fla.: Scholars' Facsimiles and Reprints, 1969. (Originally published 1805.)

Hughes, C., White, A., Sharpen, J., and Dunn, J. "Antisocial, Angry, and Unsympathetic: 'Hard-to-Manage' Preschoolers' Peer Problems and Possible Cognitive Influences." *Journal of Child Psychology and Psychiatry and Allied Disciplines,* 2000, *41,* 169–179.

Jenkins, J. M., and Astington, J. W. "Theory of Mind and Social Behavior: Causal Models Tested in a Longitudinal Study." *Merrill-Palmer Quarterly,* 2000, *46,* 203–220.

Martin, R., and Barresi, J. "Hazlitt on the Future of the Self." *Journal of the History of Ideas,* 1995, *56,* 463–481.

Meltzoff, A., and Gopnik, A. "The Role of Imitation in Understanding Persons and Developing a Theory of Mind." In S. Baron-Cohen, H. Tager-Flusberg, and D. Cohen (eds.), *Understanding Other Minds: Perspectives from Autism.* New York: Oxford University Press, 1993.

Mischel, W. "Processes in Delay of Gratification." In L. Berkowitz (ed.), *Advances in Experimental Social Psychology.* Orlando, Fla.: Academic Press, 1974.

Mischel, W., Shoda, Y., and Rodriguez, M. "Delay of Gratification in Children." *Science,* 1990, *244,* 933–938.

Moore, C., and Barresi, J. "Knowledge of the Psychological States of Self and Others Is Not Only Theory-Laden But Also Data-Driven." *Behavioral and Brain Sciences,* 1993, *16,* 61–62.

Moore, C., Barresi, J., and Thompson, C. "The Cognitive Basis of Prosocial Behavior." *Social Development,* 1998, *7,* 198–218.

Moore, C., and Frye, D. "The Acquisition and Utility of Theories of Mind." In D. Frye and C. Moore (eds.), *Children's Theories of Mind: Mental States and Social Understanding.* Mahwah, N.J.: Erlbaum, 1991.

Moore, C., and Lemmon, K. "The Nature and Utility of the Temporally Extended Self." In C. Moore and K. Lemmon (eds.), *The Self in Time: Developmental Issues.* Mahwah, N.J.: Erlbaum, 2001.

Moore, C., Pure, K., and Furrow, D. "Children's Understanding of the Modal Expression of Speaker Certainty and Uncertainty and Its Relation to the Development of a Representational Theory of Mind." *Child Development,* 1990, *61,* 722–730.

Moore, C., and Symons, D. "Social Relationships and Social Action in the Preschool Period." In B. D. Homer and C. Tamis-LeMonda (eds.), *The Development of Social Cognition and Communication.* Mahwah, N.J.: Erlbaum, forthcoming.

Povinelli, D. J. "The Unduplicated Self." In P. Rochat (ed.), *Self in Infancy: Theory and Research.* Amsterdam: North Holland-Elsevier, 1995.

Ruffman, T., Olson, D. R., Ash, T., and Keenan, T. "The ABCs of Deception: Do Young Children Understand Deception in the Same Way as Adults?" *Developmental Psychology,* 1993, *29,* 74–87.

Russell, J., Mauthner, N., Sharpe, S., and Tidswell, T. "The 'Windows Task' as a Measure of Strategic Deception in Preschoolers and Autistic Subjects." *British Journal of Developmental Psychology,* 1991, *9,* 331–349.

Shoda, Y., Mischel, W., and Peake, P. "Predicting Adolescent Cognitive and Self-

Regulatory Competencies from Preschool Delay of Gratification: Identifying Diagnostic Conditions." *Developmental Psychology,* 1989, 26, 978–986.

Slomkowski, C., and Dunn, J. "Young Children's Understanding of Other People's Beliefs and Feelings and Their Connected Communication with Friends." *Developmental Psychology,* 1996, 32, 442–447.

Thompson, C., Barresi, J., and Moore, C. "The Development of Future-Oriented Prudence and Altruism in Preschoolers." *Cognitive Development,* 1997, 12, 199–212.

CHRIS MOORE *is professor of psychology at Dalhousie University and professor and Canada Research Chair in Social Cognitive Development in the Department of Human Development and Applied Psychology at the Ontario Institute for Studies in Education of the University of Toronto.*

SHANNON MACGILLIVRAY *was a research assistant in psychology at Dalhousie University.*

The author argues that the gap between theory of mind and moral reasoning research may be more apparent than real. The wider gap is between sociomoral cognitions and real-world behavior. She calls for research on the relation of children's mental state and moral understanding to their sociomoral behavior.

Bridging the Gap Between Theory of Mind and Moral Reasoning

Janet Wilde Astington

The chapters in this volume come from a symposium designed to unite research investigating children's theory of mind, on the one hand, and sociomoral development, on the other. As Baird and Sokol argue in the Editors' Notes to this volume, because moral reasoning depends on a consideration of mental states, one would expect that children's acquisition of a theory of mind would have important consequences for their moral understanding. Baird and Sokol suggest, however, that researchers have failed to capitalize on this fundamental connection between mental life and morality. Thus, there is a gap to bridge between the two research traditions: theory-of-mind development and moral reasoning development. First, I ask why the gap exists, or rather, why it is perceived to exist, because, second, I argue that the gap may actually be more apparent than real. Nonetheless, third, I argue that there is a gap, but a different one, common to both theory-of-mind and moral reasoning research. This is a more fundamental divide that is in serious need of research attention (Dunn, 1996).

Why Is There a Gap Between Theory-of-Mind and Moral Reasoning Research?

Moral development research traces its roots back to Piaget's work on moral judgment (1965). One of Piaget's interests was in whether children assign blame to misdeeds according to objective or subjective responsibility. The

---

I am grateful to the Natural Sciences and Engineering Research Council of Canada for financial support.

former blames actions for their objective consequences, whereas the latter considers the actor's subjective mental state, specifically his or her intentions, and blames accordingly. Building on Piaget's work, Kohlberg (1969) distinguished six stages of moral reasoning, which extend from childhood into adulthood. He used stories about people faced with dilemmas involving a conflict of values; for example, in one story, the only way a protagonist can save someone's life is by stealing from someone else. Children were asked what the protagonist should do and why, and their stage of moral reasoning was determined from codings of their responses. This research shows that what is judged to be right as opposed to wrong (for example, caring for others, upholding the law) is characterized differently at different stages. Thus, moral reasoning research in the Piagetian-Kohlbergian tradition describes sequences of development based on children's evaluations of behaviors as right or wrong and their consideration of intention in justifying their judgments.

One could argue that theory-of-mind research also traces its roots back to Piaget, perhaps most particularly to his work on perspective taking (Piaget, 1926; Piaget and Inhelder, 1956). However, the links are not as strong. Indeed, in some ways, theory-of-mind research breaks with the Piagetian tradition, and its roots go back only twenty years or so. They are found in the developmental psychologist's response to the primatologist's claim that the chimpanzee has a theory of mind (Premack and Woodruff, 1978). This response centered on the now famous false-belief test (Wimmer and Perner, 1983), which shows that at about four years of age, children are able to understand that a person can hold beliefs different from their own, that is, false from their point of view, and can recognize that the person will act on the basis of the false belief. At this age, children are also able to remember their own mistaken beliefs (Gopnik and Astington, 1988). It is argued that these abilities mark a fundamental cognitive achievement: children recognize that the world is represented in mind and understand that it is people's representation of the world that determines what they say and do.

Thus, although both moral reasoning research and theory-of-mind research are concerned in some way with children's consideration of people's mental states, their emphases are different. Theory-of-mind research focuses on children's developing understanding of belief representation, particularly in the preschool years, and their conception of truth and falsity. Moral reasoning research focuses on school-aged children's rational justification of moral action, which involves consideration of intention. These differences help explain the gap between the two research traditions.

Obviously, given their brevity, these descriptions are caricatures of the two traditions, and even as caricatures, they are less apt now than they would have been just a few years ago. For example, moral reasoning researchers have recently investigated children's understanding of beliefs in relation to their moral judgments, including children as young as preschoolers (Chapter One, this volume; Wainryb and Ford, 1998). Theory-of-mind researchers are also showing more interest in moral issues as demonstrated here (Chapters Two and Three, this volume) and elsewhere (Dunn, Cutting, and Demetriou, 2000; Hughes and Dunn, 2000). In addition, within the theory-of-mind field, there has been a broadening of the age range of interest, investigating further development of belief understanding in the school-age years (Chandler and Lalonde, 1996; Kuhn, 2000). There is also more interest in children's understanding of intention as well as belief (Malle, Moses, and Baldwin, 2001; Zelazo, Astington, and Olson, 1999). All of these endeavors will help to bridge the gap—if indeed it exists, which brings me to the second question.

Is the Gap Between Theory-of-Mind and Moral Reasoning Research More Apparent than Real?

Children's theory of mind is an integrated set of mental state concepts that underlies their ability to predict, explain, and interpret human behavior (Wellman, 1990). Moral development research has a long history of concern with children's reasoning about human behavior, in particular, their evaluation of a person's actions as right or wrong, based on a consideration of his or her mental states, primarily intention. This sounds rather like theory-of-mind research, so much so, one might be tempted to argue that, like Molière's *le bourgeois gentilhomme*, who discovers he has been speaking prose all his life but did not know it, moral reasoning researchers have been doing theory-of-mind research all along. However, the obvious riposte would be that moral reasoning research predates the theory-of-mind field. How could theory of mind lay claim to moral reasoning?

Indeed, this may be an example of a more general question, or complaint—that is, as theory-of-mind research has broadened its scope, it appears to range over (some might say it appears to have taken over) most of the sociocognitive area (Flavell and Miller, 1998). However, it may be that *theory of mind* is not the right term for this research, at least not for the whole range of it. Recent years have seen more investigations of individual differences in theory-of-mind development and on the social origins and implications of theory of mind. This focus has led to different descriptions of what develops and also, importantly, to different explanations of theory-of-mind development. Some researchers argue that children do not acquire theoretical understanding, as implied by the term *theory of mind,* but rather social understanding, that is, the ability to make sense of social situations and interactions (Nelson, Plesa, and Henseler, 1998). On this view, the term *theory of mind* is an unsatisfactory substitute for *social cognition* because it leaves one in the paradoxical position of arguing that the understanding is not theoretical and is not acquired through theory construction (Nelson, Plesa, and Henseler, 1998).

However, despite the various alternative terms proposed in addition to social understanding—for example, *perspective taking, folk psychology, mindreading, mentalizing ability*—none has been generally endorsed by the research community, so *theory of mind* remains the moniker for this research area. Perhaps we should limit its range of application; that is, we should reserve the term *theory of mind* for use by those whose work presupposes that the theory of mind is a theory and is a theory that the child possesses (Astington, 1998). However, perhaps it is too late; *theory of mind* is already too widely accepted and too embedded in the literature to abolish it or to restrict its usage. Perhaps the best we can hope for is that researchers will be clear what they mean when they use the term. For some, theory of mind is as broad as almost all of social cognition, whereas for others, it is narrowly equated with the ability to pass false-belief tests. My view is somewhere in the middle ground. Children's theory of mind involves their growing awareness of an interconnected network of mental states, including belief, desire, intention, and emotion, which underlies their ability to interpret and explain human talk and action.

On this view, moral reasoning research and theory-of-mind research may well be part of the same enterprise. Theory-of-mind and moral development researchers are both concerned with how children reason about beliefs and intentions in interpreting and evaluating human action. However, the evaluation and justification of actions as right or wrong is the primary interest of moral reasoning research but is of less importance within theory-of-mind research. Nonetheless, in developing the false-belief test, Wimmer and Perner were interested in moral issues related to the development of false-belief understanding. They (Wimmer, Gruber, and Perner, 1984) adapted their original false-belief tasks—for example, the one where Maxi is out of the room when his chocolate is moved from one place to another and children are asked where he will look for it when he returns. In the adapted version, before Maxi can look for the chocolate, his sister appears and asks him where it is. In one condition, the children are told that the boy wants his sister to find the chocolate and in another condition that he does not want her to. However, he has a false belief about the location, and so in the first condition, even though he does not intend to deceive his sister, she does not find the chocolate because he has told her to look in the wrong place. In the second condition, when he does intend to deceive her, what he says is actually true because he tells her it is in the place it has been moved to, thinking it is still where he put it. Even four year olds did not blame Maxi in the first condition, but they did blame him in the second one, even though he had actually said where the chocolate was. Clearly, four year olds were making an appropriate moral judgment on the basis of intention. However, interestingly, they said that Maxi had told a lie in the first scenario, presumably because he had said something false, even though he did not know it was false and did not intend to deceive his sister. More interesting still, the connotation of the term *lie* is so strong that if children were asked the "lie" question before the moral judgment question, they were more likely to assign blame in the scenario where the boy did not intend to deceive (Wimmer, Gruber, and Perner, 1985).

Beyond this, research on children's ability to deal with doubly embedded representations (so-called second-order beliefs) has allowed theory-of-mind researchers to investigate their moral reasoning further. Perner and Wimmer (1985) showed that around seven years of age, children are able to represent and reason from second-order beliefs, for example, "He thinks that she thinks that. . . ." Such understanding may have more significance for moral reasoning than the simple recognition that someone may be mistaken about a fact of the matter in the world, because much of our social interaction depends on what people believe or intend about other people's beliefs or intentions. Indeed, the importance of second-order understanding has been shown in relation to children's ability to assign blame to lies but not to jokes or irony (Leekam, 1991; Winner and Leekam, 1991), in relation to their judgments of responsibility for accidents (Yuill and Perner, 1987), and in relation to their ability to make different moral evaluations of seemingly identical actions (Chapter Three, this volume).

Thus, my argument is that the gap between the two research traditions—theory of mind and moral reasoning—exists because theory-of-mind researchers focus on belief, especially on preschoolers' developing understanding of belief representation, whereas moral reasoning researchers focus on intention and action, especially on the evaluation of whether an action is right or wrong, in the school-age years. Importantly, however, this gap may be more a matter of emphasis than a genuine divide. Be that as it may, I agree with Baird and Sokol (Editors' Notes, this volume) and Chandler, Sokol, and Wainryb (2000) that the time is ripe to bring the two research traditions closer together, which may enrich both areas. Chandler, Sokol, and Wainryb argue that theory of mind and moral reasoning have been kept apart by a concern not to conflate matters of fact and matters of value, in deference to the philosophical edict that ethical conclusions cannot be derived from nonethical premises—the "is to ought fallacy" (Hume, 2000). Since theory of mind deals with children's understanding of true and false beliefs about matters of fact, while moral reasoning is concerned with matters of value, uniting them may unwisely conflate concern with what is and what ought to be the case. However, as Wainryb (Chapter One, this volume) points out, objective facts and subjective values are not so categorically distinct as Hume thought them to be. Indeed, Kuhn, Cheney, and Weinstock's research (2000) clearly demonstrates that beliefs about the physical world, the social world, moral values, aesthetics, and personal tastes are differently regarded as objective or subjective at different stages of development. Thus, research on theory of mind and moral reasoning would do well to integrate children's "beliefs about truth and beliefs about rightness" (Chandler, Sokol, and Wainryb, 2000, p. 91).

This is a neat way of characterizing the two fields—beliefs about truth in theory-of-mind research and beliefs about rightness in moral reasoning research—but theory-of-mind research is concerned with children's conception of truth in a way that moral reasoning research is not concerned with the conception of rightness itself. That is, the characterization overlooks the different emphases of the two fields that I have already referred to. Cryptically, one might characterize this difference as an emphasis on "what is right" versus on "what right is." Moral reasoning research is concerned with children's judgments of what is right, that is, what behaviors are right (or wrong). Theory-of-mind research is concerned with children's conception of what right is, that is, with their conception of truth (and falsity). Thus, when we are interested in belief, right-wrong applies to correctness, to truth, whereas when we are interested in action, right-wrong applies to goodness. When children first use and understand statements like, "That's right," is it in reference to behavior or to belief? It may be that the moral dimension is the more fundamental one, that is, that epistemic understanding arises from moral understanding.

Data on children's use of the term *right* are sparse. Bartsch and Wellman (1995) report that it is used in relation to truth at four years, that is, epistemically, and that it is used earlier for other purposes. Although they do not describe these other purposes, they are perhaps moral ones. In accordance with this idea that moral use precedes the epistemic one, Wells (1979, 1985) shows that the auxiliary verb system is first used for moral, deontic reference and then for epistemic reference. That is, it is first used to talk about permission and obligation and only later for possibility and inference. For example, before three years of age, children say, "You may do it," giving permission, but only a couple of years later they say, "He may do it," expressing possibility. Likewise, "He must come in," expressing obligation, precedes by several years, "He must be cold," expressing inference. That is, although they are using the same auxiliary verbs in the same syntactic frames, children express deontic modality some years before epistemic modality. The latter, expressing the relative certainty of the speaker's knowledge, is associated with the development of false-belief understanding (Moore, Pure, and Furrow, 1990).

Similarly, there is evidence that reasoning in the moral domain precedes epistemic reasoning. Cummins (1996) showed that three and four year olds were capable of deontic reasoning before they were successful at a comparable epistemic reasoning task. In the task, identical-looking mice were in the house and the backyard, some could squeak and some could not (the only way to tell them apart was to squeeze them), and further, it was not safe for the squeaky mice to be outside because the cat would get them. In the deontic condition, a puppet told children, "It's not safe outside for the squeaky mice, so all squeaky mice must stay in the house," and they were asked which mice must be tested—those in the house or those outside—to ensure that no one had disobeyed. In the epistemic condition, the puppet told children, "It's not safe outside for the squeaky mice, so all squeaky mice are in the house," and they were asked which mice must be tested—those in the house or those outside—to see if what the puppet said was true. In both cases, the correct response is to test the mice in the backyard to ensure there are no squeaky ones there. Results showed that the deontic task was considerably easier: two-thirds of three year olds and a large majority of four year olds responded correctly, whereas in the epistemic task, only a third of three and four year olds were correct. Essentially the task sets up a contrast between "doing it right" and "saying it right," and children find it easier to judge the action, where "right" refers to obedience, than the statement, where "right" refers to truth.

My general point here is that a fruitful way of bridging the gap between the two research traditions may be by investigating the developmental relationship between them. However, a second way is by conducting investigations that are designed to bridge what is a more fundamental gap, one that is common to both theory-of-mind and moral reasoning research.

The More Fundamental Gap

The shared concern of the chapters in this volume is the interface between theory of mind and sociomoral development, between mind, morals, and action. There are actually two interfaces here. First, there is the one between mind and morals, which I have already discussed, concluding that although there are questions of how the two research traditions can be brought closer together, the issues that they address are similar in many ways. The second interface is the one between mind and action and also between morals and action. That is, it is the interface between reasoning and behavior, and it is the same issue in theory-of-mind and in moral development research. What the relation is between social cognition and social behavior is a similar question to what the relation is between moral reasoning and moral behavior. This interface between cognitions and behaviors is the more fundamental, more interesting, and more difficult one, which the chapters here go some way toward addressing.

An important part of Baird and Astington's study (Chapter Three, this volume) is the investigation of relations between children's judgments on the motives task and their social behavior as reported by their teachers. We found that physically aggressive children were less able to use mental state information in evaluating the behavior of the story characters in the motives task. This is consistent with Dodge's work (1980) showing that aggressive children have more difficulty interpreting others' intentions. Thus, it may be that understanding others' mental states contributes to appropriate social behavior.

However, as Moore and Macgillivray (Chapter Four, this volume) point out at the end of their chapter, possessing an understanding of another's mental state is only part of the reason that one might empathize with and try to help or comfort the other. That is, as well as understanding their needs, one also has to have the motivation to help. Thus, knowing that a child has an understanding of others' beliefs and intentions is not sufficient to predict how he or she will behave in real social situations.

Moore and Macgillivray are referring here to the psychologists' prediction of children's behaviors. Analogously, Sokol, Chandler, and Jones (Chapter Two, this volume) argue that in our everyday lives, we do not mechanistically explain and predict human activity but rather we try to understand and interpret it. Thus, just as for the scientist, so for the child, understanding a person's beliefs and intentions is insufficient to interpret their behavior in the real world. In order to do this, we have to consider the whole person as a free agent whose motives to help or to harm operate in conjunction with their cognitive understanding of people's mental states.

The analysis in Chapter Two by Sokol, Chandler, and Jones draws attention to the complexity of people's actions and interactions in the real world, which cannot be as simply predicted and explained as theory of mind or belief-desire psychology might have us think. Wainryb's methods and findings (Chapter One, this volume), showing how children's understanding of the diversity of people's beliefs influences their moral judgments, provide a way to investigate children's understanding of the complexities of social interaction within the real world. Children's tolerance of beliefs and practices different from their own may depend on their developing understanding of the subjectivity and diversity of beliefs. Indeed, developing such understanding may be a more important route to encouraging tolerance than educators' practice of exposing children to the customs of different cultural groups (Wainryb, Shaw, and Maianu, 1998).

To conclude, over the past two decades, research in theory of mind has revealed a great deal about children's understanding of the mental states underlying people's behavior. During this period and earlier, moral reasoning research has shown how children use their mental state understanding in judging people's behavior. The time is ripe to look at interrelations in the development of mental state and moral understanding. Furthermore, and perhaps more important, we need to investigate the relation of this understanding to children's social behavior in the real world.

References

Astington, J. W. "Theory of Mind, Humpty Dumpty, and the Icebox." *Human Development,* 1998, *41,* 30–39.

Bartsch, K., and Wellman, H. M. *Children Talk About the Mind.* New York: Oxford University Press, 1995.

Chandler, M., and Lalonde, C. "Shifting to an Interpretive Theory of Mind: Five- to Seven-Year-Olds' Changing Conceptions of Mental Life." In A. J. Sameroff and M. M. Haith (eds.), *The Five to Seven Year Shift: The Age of Reason and Responsibility.* Chicago: University of Chicago Press, 1996.

Chandler, M. J., Sokol, B. W., and Wainryb, C. "Beliefs About Truth and Beliefs About Rightness." *Child Development,* 2000, *71,* 91–97.

Cummins, D. D. "Evidence of Deontic Reasoning in Three- and Four-Year-Old Children." *Memory and Cognition,* 1996, *24,* 823–829.

Dodge, K. A. "Social Cognition and Children's Aggressive Behavior." *Child Development*, 1980, *51*, 162–170.

Dunn, J. "Children's Relationships: Bridging the Divide Between Cognitive and Social Development." *Journal of Child Psychology and Psychiatry*, 1996, *37*, 507–518.

Dunn, J., Cutting, A. L., and Demetriou, H. "Moral Sensibility, Understanding Others, and Children's Friendship Interactions in the Preschool Period." *British Journal of Developmental Psychology*, 2000, *18*, 159–177.

Flavell, J. H., and Miller, P. H. "Social Cognition." In W. Damon (series ed.), D. Kuhn and R. Siegler (vol. eds.), *Handbook of Child Psychology: Vol. 2: Cognition, Perception and Language*. (5th ed.) New York: Wiley, 1998.

Gopnik, A., and Astington, J. W. "Children's Understanding of Representational Change and Its Relation to the Understanding of False Belief and the Appearance-Reality Distinction." *Child Development*, 1988, *59*, 26–37.

Hughes, C., and Dunn, J. "Hedonism or Empathy? Hard-to-Manage Children's Moral Awareness and Links with Cognitive and Maternal Characteristics." *British Journal of Developmental Psychology*, 2000, *18*, 227–245.

Hume, D. *A Treatise of Human Nature* (D. F. Norton and M. J. Norton, eds.). New York: Oxford University Press, 2000. (Originally published 1739.)

Kohlberg, L. "Stage and Sequence: The Cognitive-Developmental Approach to Socialization." In D. A. Goslin (ed.), *Handbook of Socialization Theory and Research*. Skokie, Ill.: Rand McNally, 1969.

Kuhn, D. "Theory of Mind, Metacognition, and Reasoning: A Life-Span Perspective." In P. Mitchell and K. J. Riggs (eds.), *Children's Reasoning and the Mind*. Hove: Psychology Press, 2000.

Kuhn, D., Cheney, R., and Weinstock, M. "The Development of Epistemological Understanding." *Cognitive Development*, 2000, *15*, 309–328.

Leekam, S. R. "Jokes and Lies: Children's Understanding of Intentional Falsehood." In A. Whiten (ed.), *Natural Theories of Mind: Evolution, Development and Simulation of Everyday Mindreading*. Oxford: Blackwell, 1991.

Malle, B. F., Moses, L. J., and Baldwin, D. A. (eds.). *Intentions and Intentionality: Foundations of Social Cognition*. Cambridge, Mass.: MIT Press, 2001.

Moore, C., Pure, K., and Furrow, D. "Children's Understanding of the Modal Expressions of Speaker Certainty and Uncertainty and Its Relation to the Development of a Representational Theory of Mind." *Child Development*, 1990, *61*, 722–730.

Nelson, K., Plesa, D., and Henseler, S. "Children's Theory of Mind: An Experiential Interpretation." *Human Development*, 1998, *41*, 7–29.

Perner, J., and Wimmer, H. "'John *Thinks* That Mary *Thinks* That. . . .': Attribution of Second-Order Beliefs by Five- to Ten-Year-Old Children." *Journal of Experimental Child Psychology*, 1985, *39*, 437–471.

Piaget, J. *The Language and Thought of the Child* (M. Gabain, trans.). London: Kegan Paul, 1926. (Originally published 1923.)

Piaget, J. *The Moral Judgment of the Child* (M. Gabain, trans.). New York: Free Press, 1965. (Originally published 1932.)

Piaget, J., and Inhelder, B. *The Child's Conception of Space* (F. J. Langdon and J. L. Lunzer, trans.). London: Routledge and Kegan Paul, 1956. (Originally published 1948.)

Premack, D., and Woodruff, G. "Does the Chimpanzee Have a Theory of Mind?" *Behavioral and Brain Sciences*, 1978, *1*, 515–526.

Wainryb, C., and Ford, S. "Young Children's Evaluations of Acts Based on Beliefs Different from Their Own." *Merrill-Palmer Quarterly*, 1998, *44*, 484–503.

Wainryb, C., Shaw, L. A., and Maianu, C. "Tolerance and Intolerance: Children's and Adolescents' Judgments of Dissenting Beliefs, Speech, Persons, and Conduct." *Child Development*, 1998, *69*, 1541–1555.

Wellman, H. M. *The Child's Theory of Mind*. Cambridge, Mass.: MIT Press, 1990.

Wells, G. "Learning and Using the Auxiliary Verb in English." In V. Lee (ed.), *Language Development*. London: Croom Helm, 1979.

Wells, G. *Language Development in the Pre-school Years*. Cambridge: Cambridge University Press, 1985.

Wimmer, H., Gruber, S., and Perner, J. "Young Children's Conception of Lying: Lexical Realism—Moral Subjectivism." *Journal of Experimental Child Psychology*, 1984, 37, 1–30.

Wimmer, H., Gruber, S., and Perner, J. "Young Children's Conception of Lying: Moral Intuition and the Denotation and Connotation of 'to Lie'." *Developmental Psychology*, 1985, 21, 993–995.

Wimmer, H., and Perner, J. "Beliefs About Beliefs: Representation and Constraining Function of Wrong Beliefs in Young Children's Understanding of Deception." *Cognition*, 1983, 13, 103–128.

Winner, E., and Leekam, S. "Distinguishing Irony from Deception: Understanding the Speaker's Second-Order Intention." *British Journal of Developmental Psychology*, 1991, 9, 257–270.

Yuill, N., and Perner, J. "Exceptions to Mutual Trust: Children's Use of Second-order Beliefs in Responsibility Attribution." *International Journal of Behavioral Development*, 1987, 10, 207–223.

Zelazo, P. D., Astington, J. W., and Olson, D. R. (eds.). *Developing Theories of Intention: Social Understanding and Self-Control*. Mahwah, N.J.: Erlbaum, 1999.

JANET WILDE ASTINGTON *is professor and chair of the Department of Human Development and Applied Psychology at the Ontario Institute for Studies in Education of the University of Toronto.*

6

The author suggests that theory of mind can help the moral developmental field uncover children's concepts of persons and psychological systems. Conversely, moral developmental theory can help theory of mind move toward nonreductionistic theorizing and research.

Mind and Morality

Peter H. Kahn Jr.

It is puzzling that the fields of theory of mind and oral development have remained largely divided over the years. Is the reason mostly due to their different starting points, or to an academic culture that rewards novelty? Or as Sokol, Chandler, and Jones (Chapter Two, this volume) suggest, are there fundamental theoretical disagreements that make bridging these two fields difficult? In this commentary, I provide some theoretical, historical, and personal perspective on these questions. By discussing the chapters, I hope to further the integrative goals of this timely volume.

Theory of Mind and Computational Conceptions of the Mind

Sokol, Chandler, and Jones (Chapter Two, this volume) argue that theory of mind has "promoted an impoverished conception of agency that, in the end, proves to be incompatible with day-to-day conceptions of mind and morality." I would like to unpack this idea and offer a slightly different conclusion.

First, let us get a sense of why people like ourselves ("folk") might have conceptions of morality. Imagine three situations. In the first situation, a man is walking in the woods, alongside some craggy cliffs. A boulder dislodges from the ledges above, plummets down, and kills the man. As unfortunate as this situation is for the man, we would not normally say that the boulder acted immorally. In the second situation, a man is walking in the woods, and a mountain lion pounces out from the trees and kills the man (and feeds her

---

I thank Stephanie Carlson and Charles Helwig for comments on an earlier version of this chapter.

cubs with him). Again, from the man's standpoint, this situation is most unfortunate. But we would not normally say that the lion acted immorally, even though the lion is a biological animal (and some readers might even say has intentions and desires). In the third situation, a man is walking in the woods, and a bandit, with a knife in hand, steals the man's money and on parting kills him. It is only in this last situation that we would normally say something unethical or immoral has occurred. Why do we say this? Presumably it is because we believe that morality involves not only intentions and desires, but intentions and desires of a certain type—for example, desires for human well-being and for fairness and justice in social relationships. We also believe that morality involves a significant measure of free choice, such that people can be held responsible for their actions.

Sokol, Chandler, and Jones point out in Chapter Two that the psychological fields have a long history of dismissing such folk conceptions of morality. B. F. Skinner, for example, who for decades helped chart the behavioristic course of psychology, believed that moral (or immoral) acts have no more "moral" (or "immoral") epistemic standing than any other human act. As Skinner (1971) wrote, "Relevant social contingencies are implied by 'You ought not to steal,' which could be translated, 'If you tend to avoid punishment, avoid stealing,' or 'Stealing is wrong, and wrong behavior is punished.' Such a statement is no more normative than 'If coffee keeps you awake when you want to go to sleep, don't drink it'" (p. 114). It is for such reasons that Skinner titled the above referenced book *Beyond Freedom and Dignity*. He could have as equally well titled this book (or another) *Beyond Morality*.

In recent decades, scientific psychological theories have similarly drawn on nonmoral conceptions of the human mind, particularly by employing mechanistic metaphors. Cosmides, Tooby, and Barkow (1992), for example, write of "information-processing mechanisms situated in human minds" (p. 3) and of the brain as "a computer made out of organic compounds" (p. 8). Pinker (1997) argues "that the mind is a system of organs of computation designed by natural selection to solve the problems faced by our evolutionary ancestors in their foraging way of life" (p. x). Dawkins (1976) says, "We are survival machines—robot vehicles blindly programmed to preserve the selfish molecules known as genes" (p. ix).

Such analogies between the human mind and machine are particularly perplexing when we broach the subject of morality. By most accounts, machines are not moral agents. If we are machines, wherein lies our moral agency? Of course, at times, it may be useful to think of the human mind as if it were a piece of computational machinery. But as Searle (1990) notes, while it can be useful to model water molecules with Ping-Pong balls in a bathtub, no one jumps into a bathtub of Ping-Pong balls expecting to get wet. Similarly, in our computational modeling, we should not confuse mind with machine. The point that Sokol, Chandler, and Jones make is that theory of mind does just that.

Are they correct? I think the answer depends on what one reads in the theory-of-mind literature and, even then, whether one takes the words at face value. For example, Gopnik, Meltzoff, and Kuhl (1999) write:

> Babies are a kind of very special computer. They are computers made of neurons, instead of silicon chips, and programmed by evolution, instead of by guys with pocket protectors. They take input from the world, the flickering chaos of sensations, and they (and therefore we) somehow turn it into jokes, apologies, tables, and spoons. Our job as developmental psychologists is to discover what program babies run and, someday, how that program is coded in their brains and how it evolved [p. 6].

Later, Gopnik, Meltzoff, and Kuhl (1999) write, "The Big Idea, the conceptual breakthrough of the last thirty years of psychology, is that the brain is a kind of computer. That's the basis of the new field of cognitive science" (p. 21). Yet even when theory-of-mind researchers employ strong computational language, it is hard to believe that they would vouch for its reductionist and mechanistic implications. After all, their research publications are filled with rich, nuanced accounts of the child's interpretative and intentional stance. Such accounts seem incompatible with a conception of the child as a programmed, nonmoral automaton.

That said, I think we need to heed the message from Sokol, Chandler, and Jones in Chapter Two. The theory-of-mind metaphor of the mind as computer needs to be more carefully articulated to better support concepts of meaning, morality, and free will. The theory-of-mind computational framework also needs to account for how individuals can shape, from an ethical stance, cultural practices. These are not easy tasks. Thus, one of the strengths of this volume is that it draws on the moral-developmental literature, and especially the "domain-specific" approach to moral development, to help ground the moral underpinnings of theory of mind.

The Domain-Specific Approach to Moral Development: Historical and Personal Reflections

The domain-specific approach to moral development emerged more than two decades ago, in part as a correction to Kohlberg's theory that views moral development in terms of increasing differentiation. According to Kohlberg (1969, 1971), through development, moral judgments pull away from personal concerns (stages 1 and 2) and then conventional concerns (stages 3 and 4) before achieving the generalizable and universal features of principled moral reasoning (stages 5 and 6). Yet according to domain theorists, one problem with such an account is that it underestimates the ways in which even young children construct distinctly moral judgments.

For example, suppose we ask a seven-year-old child, "Is it all right or not all right for Sally to push Joan off the swing because Sally wants to swing?" The child might initially provide a Kohlbergian-looking stage 1 response: "No, that's not all right because Sally could get in trouble." But then say we counter-probed with any number of different questions. We ask the child, "Let's say Sally wouldn't get in trouble. Would it then be all right or not all right?" Or we ask, "Let's say the rule at Sally's school says that if you want to push, it's up to you. Would it then be all right or not all right?" Or we ask, "Let's say that in another school [or country], the way they did things there is it's up to the child whether he or she wants to push. Would it be all right or not all right for children in that school [or country] to push in this sort of situation?" What domain theorists have found is that for all such questions, children typically respond, "It's still not all right," and children typically base their judgments on considerations of neither fear of punishment nor conventional practices, but human welfare (for example, "because Joan could get hurt") or fairness (for example, "it's not fair, because Joan was swinging first, and Sally should just wait her turn"). More formally, Turiel (1983) says that such questions (that elicit what he calls criterion judgments) establish conceptual boundaries for the moral domain, based on the criteria of prescriptivity, rule contingency, and generalizability (and supporting welfare and fairness justifications). Based on these criteria, domain theorists have provided convincing evidence that even young children bring forward distinctively moral judgments (for reviews, see Smetana, 1995; Tisak, 1995; Turiel, 1998).

During the early 1980s, I was beginning my graduate work in moral development. Part of what I found particularly powerful about the domain-specific approach was that it sought to place moral judgments within a larger developmental framework. For example, in his 1983 volume, *The Development of Social Knowledge,* Turiel lays out a research agenda:

> The analyses and documentation presented in this volume provide the foundation for extending.... the domain-specific interpretation of structure and development to a more general theoretical framework regarding social development.... On the basis of the assumption that the individual's social world includes other persons, relations between persons, and institutionalized systems of social interaction, it is proposed that the child's structuring of the social world revolves around three general categories. These are (1) concepts of persons or psychological systems (the psychological domain), (2) conceptions of systems of social relations and organizations (the societal domain) of which convention is but one component, and (3) prescriptive judgments of justice, rights, and welfare (the moral domain) [pp. 3–4].

Thus, according to Turiel, moral judgments need to be understood within the context of three domains of social knowledge: the moral, social-conventional, and psychological.

At the time, the psychological domain (which involved "concepts of persons or psychological systems") was understood to include children's concepts of agency and intentionality—a version of what has become known as a theory of mind. Thus, I thought domain theorists were particularly well poised for the integration of psychological, social, and moral reasoning—for creating a unified theory, if you will, of social development. In subsequent years, however, the psychological domain became blurred with the personal domain: concepts that pertain to individual authority and focus on actions (for example, one's choice of friends and recreational activities) that often lie outside the realm of justifiable social regulation (Nucci, 1981, 1996). I was puzzled at the time, wondering if perhaps the personal domain could be thought of as a subset of the psychological domain; but I did not worry unduly because I figured it would all be straightened out in due course. But it has not been. While Nucci (2001) and others continue to make important contributions to the field based on analyses of personal reasoning, an account of the psychological domain has not been developed.

During this period that started in the 1980s, others from the domain perspective and I were certainly aware that another area in psychological research was starting to emerge, called theory of mind. At the time, I (and others) thought theory of mind was emerging from too narrow an empirical basis (for example, the false-belief task) and driven by what seemed to be quick publishable experiments. And like Sokol, Chandler, and Jones (Chapter Two, this volume), I thought theory of mind seemed rooted to a computational conception of the mind that would prevent serious engagement with and theorizing about the moral life. Since then, theory of mind has perhaps mined most of what is possible from the false-belief paradigm and is now broadening into areas of biology, culture, and, as evidenced from this volume, moral development. What can the shape of such research look like?

New Directions for Theory of Mind and Moral Development

The contributors to this volume take up this question head on. Baird and Astington (Chapter Three) stake out a key area of research for the field today: investigating children's ability to consider intentions in judging the moral quality of others' actions. This distinction between moral intention and action is crucial in moral theorizing, our courts of law, and, of course, our common judgments. After all, say I told you, "Bob spends every Saturday at his aunt's house, helping her with chores." You might think, "Oh, what a wonderful person Bob is." Then I tell you, "Bob helps his aunt only because the aunt is rich and old and close to death, and Bob hopes to inherit it all." Then you might think, "Well, Bob's not quite the moral guy I thought he was." In other words, it matters why we do the things we do.

Such investigations into conceptions of moral intentions and consequences have a long history in the moral-developmental literature (Piaget, 1965). Against this backdrop, Baird and Astington sought to vary intentions ("good" versus "bad") while keeping the act (for example, turning on a garden hose) identical. Their results suggest that both four and five year olds can evaluate and punish differently on the basis of the actor's intentions. I suspect Baird and Astington's conclusion is correct (Helwig, Hildebrandt, and Turiel, 1995), but I am less convinced by the methodical design of the study. Baird and Astington sought to use a "neutral" stimulus (such as turning on a garden hose) that could then be paired with a "good" intention (such as helping one's mother water the garden) and "bad" intention (such as ruining a sibling's sand castle). But it is not clear to me that the "neutral" action can be severed from the "good" and "bad" actions that follow. In other words, when a child is reasoning about the events, it seems likely he or she is considering not only two different intentions and the "neutral" action but two different consequences, and that those consequences are wrapped up in the evaluation of the seemingly neutral action. Granted, Baird and Astington did not provide children with information about consequences; thus, for my interpretation to be correct, children would have to be inferring or creating consequences on their own. But if the children did, then Baird and Astington's experimental design may not allow for the precision that they seek in their interpretation.

In future investigations, I would also add two other pointers from the moral developmental side. If one wants to examine moral reasoning, it is important to employ moral stimuli. Is helping one's mother water a garden moral? Perhaps it is in a morally "discretionary" sense (Kahn, 1992, 1997, 2002) but not in the classic moral sense by which domain theorists understand the term. Similarly, when seeking moral evaluations, it is usually not enough to garner judgments of "good" versus "bad." After all, people also make judgments that many types of nonmoral violations are bad (or good). For example, many people would say that it is "bad" to eat a baked potato with your fingers at a fancy restaurant, but only because of conventional (not moral) expectations. It is for this reason that domain theorists employ criterion judgments (discussed above) coupled with justification data. Baird and Astington move in this direction with their assessments of moral culpability (punishment).

Like Baird and Astington, Moore and Macgillivray (Chapter Four) stake out a rich area for investigation. They are interested in how a child's psychological understanding of self and others (theory of mind) can help regulate the child's own moral behavior. They report on a series of studies wherein they employed delay-of-gratification tasks. For example, one task involves a game wherein a child was offered one sticker now or two stickers at the end of the game. A second (no-cost sharing) task involved a choice between one sticker now for self and two stickers now shared between the two players. In other manipulations, Moore and Macgillivray investigated what they call "simple sharing with cost" (two stickers now or one apiece now), "delayed sharing" (two stickers for self now or one each later), and "future-oriented prudence" (one sticker for self now or two for self later). Through such manipulations, Moore and Macgillivray sought to understand the sources of variation for sharing (for example, developmental or individual differences) and the relationship between prosocial behavior and prudence. Taken together, they also discuss how prudence and prosocial behavior relate to theory of mind.

Moore and Macgillivray ask good questions and are sensitive to the complexity of their results. I would ask one further question: How does all of this (prudence, prosocial behavior, and theory of mind) relate to moral development? A likely answer is that prosocial behavior is the moral component. But some time ago, it was clear to many in the field that *prosocial behavior* is a broad term that can refer to both moral and nonmoral acts (Smetana, Bridgeman, and Turiel, 1983). Moreover, we need to remember Baird and Astington's earlier point: to establish the moral basis of an act, the moral description needs to include both behavior and reasoning. Consider another example. Imagine that Jane walks past a homeless person on the street who asks her for money. Is Jane's response immoral behavior? Is it nonmoral behavior? Well, what were Jane's reasons? Maybe she saw the homeless man drinking alcohol and worried that giving the man money would lead to his further deterioration. Maybe she actually knew the man and believed that he was making a choice to be on the street and could successfully gain employment if he so chose. Or say that Jane does give the homeless man money. Maybe she does so only out of fear that otherwise the homeless man will assault her. Or maybe she believes that a person should not walk past another human being in need without somehow recognizing their dignity, and in this context money is the mechanism for conveying her recognition. The point is that children too bring complex assessments of context and moral judgments to bear in their social and moral reasoning, even in laboratory contexts. Thus, it would be good (in the nonmoral sense, of course) to assess such reasons and then to integrate them into further analyses of social competence and theory of mind.

Drawing on the domain-specific approach, Wainryb (Chapter One) provides empirical support for the proposition that children can arrive at different moral decisions because of a dispute over not their moral beliefs but factual beliefs. An important implication follows for cross-cultural investigations. To explicate how, consider Shweder, Mahapatra, and Miller's data (1987) that show that devout Hindus believe that it is immoral for menstruating women to sleep in the same beds as their husbands. When Turiel, Killen, and Helwig (1987) reexamined the data, they found that devout Hindus believe that menstrual blood is poisonous and harmful to husbands. In such a situation, devout Hindus and traditional Westerners presumably share the moral belief that wives should care for the well-being of their husbands. Where they differ is in the factual belief about what causes harm. Thus, Wainryb's research helps check anthropologists (and many laypeople, as well) who too often jump to the conclusion that when cultures differ in their practices, the cultures also differ substantively in their moral judgments.

Wainryb also offers some provocative connections to theory of mind, since she too is interested in false beliefs. Indeed, Wainryb suggests that false beliefs may be better categorized in at least two ways. In one way, a false belief can be understood as a mistaken belief. For example, her four-year-old daughter, Julia, held a mistaken belief that a person can see every type of bug ("Of course, there are no bugs that *no one* can see"). In a second way, the false belief can be understood as a belief that others can have legitimate grounds for an alternative interpretation of reality. For example, while a person may not believe that spanking a child is pedagogically desirable, he or she can recognize that others might and (with limits) perhaps give some ground to such behavior. Like Sokol, Chandler, and Jones in Chapter Two and their colleagues (Carpendale and Chandler, 1996; Chandler and Lalonde, 1996), Wainryb has found that children's understanding that others can have alternative interpretations comes later than the understanding that others can have mistaken beliefs.

In such ways, Wainryb offers a powerful and innovative approach to investigating social judgments. Indeed, I draw on her work frequently in my own research and theorizing (Kahn, 1999; Kahn and Lourenço, 1999). Yet over the years, I have also wondered whether one can completely disentangle moral beliefs from factual beliefs. As a case in point, consider the factual belief of a nineteenth-century American, R. R. Cobb, when he was addressing the issue of slavery: "A state of bondage, so far from doing violence to the law of nature, develops and perfects it; and that, in that state (the Negro) enjoys the greatest amount of happiness, and arrives at the greatest degree of perfection, of which his nature is capable" (quoted in Spiegel, 1988, p. 39). Let us imagine we challenged Cobb. We might say: "Mr. Cobb, you are an immoral person." Cobb might respond: "You are mistaken. I care very much for the welfare of human beings, and always treat humans with respect and dignity. But the fact is that Negroes are not fully human, and thus (like animals) are not accorded the same moral standing as humans." With such reasoning at hand and Wainryb's distinction employed, we could then be left saying, "Mr. Cobb, isn't it interesting that we actually share the same moral beliefs and differ only regarding our factual assumptions." While there is something right about this statement, there seems to me something wrong about it as well, insofar as some factual beliefs appear so morally laden that to get them wrong implicates one's moral life.

Wainryb is aware of such potential difficulties and moves deftly to address them. For example, she recognizes that people may on occasion deliberately or unconsciously conceal what they believe to be true as a means to advance personal goals or to evade inner conflict. Yet Wainryb, I think correctly, argues that such rationalization does not characterize the central unit of analysis in the moral life.

Wainryb also responds to the potential charge that her position could be construed as morally relativistic. She writes, for example, "We maintain that through different construals or understandings of the facts of reality any act can be judged as morally wrong, but only insofar as the facts are understood to signal the presence of intentional harm. This is not akin to saying, as moral relativists do, that the relation between act and moral judgment is arbitrary" (cf. Wainryb, 2000). Yet here I am not convinced that Wainryb can give up so much initial ground (that "any act can be judged as immoral") and still maintain (by means of an individual's perception or judgment of "intentional harm") a firm nonarbitrary connection between act and moral judgment. After all, individuals sometimes differ in their perception or judgment of when intentional harm occurs. Moreover, what checks the "Mr. Cobb" scenario above, where construals of reality (factual beliefs) transform seemingly immoral acts (slavery) into nonmoral acts? In such ways, there is a greater amount of moral relativism embedded in Wainryb's current position than most domain theorists (Wainryb included) have proposed in the past.

Conclusion

From this small volume lies the potential for the fields of theory of mind and moral development to enrich one another. Theory of mind can help moral-developmental domain researchers fulfill the original promise of the psychological domain, uncovering children's concepts of persons and psychological systems. From such work, it would then be possible to develop a more unified theory of social development. Conversely, domain theory can help move theory of mind toward nonreductionistic theorizing and research. But for this move to succeed, moral beliefs need to be viewed within theory of mind not as epiphenomenal (as mere "folk" conceptions, in the way that "natives" might have folk conceptions that the world is flat), but as playing an epistemically valid and psychologically authentic role in human lives. As a first step, the contributors to this volume have established an important dialogue between the fields of theory of mind and moral development. Perhaps fruitful empirical collaborations will follow.

References

Carpendale, J. I., and Chandler, M. J. "On the Distinction Between False Belief Understanding and Subscribing to an Interpretive Theory of Mind." *Child Development,* 1996, 67, 1686–1706.

Chandler, M. J., and Lalonde, C. "Shifting from an Interpretive Theory of Mind: Five- to Seven-Year-Olds' Changing Conceptions of Mental Life." In A. J. Sameroff and M. M. Haith (eds.), *The Five to Seven Year Shift: The Age of Reason and Responsibility.* Chicago: University of Chicago Press, 1996.

Cosmides, L., Tooby, J., and Barkow, J. H. "Introduction: Evolutionary Psychology and Conceptual Integration." In J. H. Barkow, L. Cosmides, and J. Tooby (eds.), *The*

Adapted Mind: Evolutionary Psychology and the Generation of Culture. New York: Oxford University Press, 1992.

Dawkins, R. *The Selfish Gene.* New York: Oxford University Press, 1976.

Gopnik, A., Meltzoff, A. N., and Kuhl, P. K. *The Scientist in the Crib: What Early Learning Tells Us About the Mind.* New York: Morrow, 1999.

Helwig, C. C., Hildebrandt, C., and Turiel, E. "Children's Judgments About Psychological Harm in Social Context." *Child Development,* 1995, 66, 1680–1693.

Kahn, P. H., Jr. "Children's Obligatory and Discretionary Moral Judgments." *Child Development,* 1992, 63, 416–430.

Kahn, P. H., Jr. "Children's Moral and Ecological Reasoning About the Prince William Sound Oil Spill." *Developmental Psychology,* 1997, 33, 1091–1096.

Kahn, P. H., Jr. *The Human Relationship with Nature: Development and Culture.* Cambridge, Mass.: MIT Press, 1999.

Kahn, P. H., Jr. "Children's Affiliations with Nature: Structure, Development, and the Problem of Environmental Generational Amnesia." In P. H. Kahn Jr. and S. R. Kellert (eds.), *Children and Nature: Psychological, Sociocultural, and Evolutionary Investigations.* Cambridge, Mass.: MIT Press, 2002.

Kahn, P. H., Jr., and Lourenço, O. "Reinstating Modernity in Social Science Research—or—The Status of Bullwinkle in a Post-Postmodern Era." *Human Development,* 1999, 42, 92–108.

Kohlberg, L. "Stage and Sequence: The Cognitive-Developmental Approach to Socialization." In D. A. Goslin (ed.), *Handbook of Socialization Theory and Research.* Skokie, Ill.: Rand McNally, 1969.

Kohlberg, L. "From Is to Ought: How to Commit the Naturalistic Fallacy and Get Away with It in the Study of Moral Development." In T. Mischel (ed.), *Cognitive Development and Epistemology.* Orlando, Fla.: Academic Press, 1971.

Nucci, L. P. "The Development of Personal Concepts: A Domain Distinct from Moral and Societal Concepts." *Child Development,* 1981, 52, 114–121.

Nucci, L. P. "Morality and the Personal Sphere of Actions." In E. S. Reed, E. Turiel, and T. Brown (eds.), *Values and Knowledge.* Mahwah, N.J.: Erlbaum, 1996.

Nucci, L. P. *Education in the Moral Domain.* Cambridge: Cambridge University Press, 2001.

Piaget, J. *The Moral Judgment of the Child* (M. Gabain, trans.). New York: Free Press, 1965. (Originally published 1932.)

Pinker, S. *How the Mind Works.* New York: Norton, 1997.

Searle, J. R. "Is the Brain's Mind a Computer Program?" *Scientific American,* 1990, 262, 26–31.

Shweder, R. A., Mahapatra, M., and Miller, J. B. "Culture and Moral Development." In J. Kagan and S. Lamb (eds.), *The Emergence of Morality in Young Children.* Chicago: University of Chicago Press, 1987.

Skinner, B. F. *Beyond Freedom and Dignity.* New York: Knopf, 1971.

Smetana, J. G. "Morality in Context: Abstractions, Ambiguities and Applications." In R. Vasta (ed.), *Annals of Child Development.* London: Jessica Kingsley, 1995.

Smetana, J. G., Bridgeman, D. L., and Turiel, E. "Differentiation of Domains and Prosocial Behavior." In D. L. Bridgeman (ed.), *The Nature of Prosocial Development.* Orlando, Fla.: Academic Press, 1983.

Spiegel, M. *The Dreaded Comparison: Human and Animal Slavery.* New York: Mirror Books, 1988.

Tisak, M. S. "Domains of Social Reasoning and Beyond." In R. Vasta (ed.), *Annals of Child Development.* London: Jessica Kingsley, 1995.

Turiel, E. *The Development of Social Knowledge.* Cambridge: Cambridge University Press, 1983.

Turiel, E. "The Development of Morality." In W. Damon (series ed.) and N. Eisenberg (vol. ed.), *Handbook of Child Psychology: Vol. 3. Social, Emotional, and Personality Development* (5th ed.). New York: Wiley, 1998.

Turiel, E., Killen, M., and Helwig, C. C. "Morality: Its Structure, Functions and Vagaries." In J. Kagan and S. Lamb (eds.), *The Emergence of Morality in Young Children*. Chicago: University of Chicago Press, 1987.

Wainryb, C. "Values and Truths: The Making and Judging of Moral Decisions." In M. Laupa (ed.), *Rights and Wrongs: How Children and Young Adults Evaluate the World*. New Directions for Child and Adolescent Development, no. 89. San Francisco: Jossey-Bass, 2000.

PETER H. KAHN JR. *is research associate professor of psychology at the University of Washington, adjunct research associate professor in the Information School at the University of Washington, and codirector of the Mina Institute in Covelo, California.*

Index

Abortion, 6
Actions: in belief-desire psychology, 23; definition of, 19, 23; and intentions, 30; link between moral reasoning and morality of, 43–47
Adams, P., 12
Adolescents: interplay of factual and moral beliefs in, 5–9; tolerance of others' beliefs by, 13
Agency: in contemporary psychological thought, 19–20; and current theory of mind literature, 22–23; and interpretive theory of mind, 26–32; in older versus younger children, 24–25, 26; passive conception of, 24–25, 33; and praise and blame, 26–29; research problems with, 23
Aggressive children, 43–45
Altruism: definition of, 51, 52; historical considerations of, 52; and theory of mind, 53–60; versus prudence, 52
Angelopoulos, M., 46
Anscombe, G.E.M., 3
Antisocial behavior, 52
Asch, S. E., 5, 7
Ash, T., 52
Astington, J. W., 21, 29, 30, 37, 44, 52, 53, 58, 63, 64, 65, 66, 77, 78
Auxillary verb system, 68

Baird, J. A., 2, 37–38, 39, 43, 77, 78
Baldwin, D. A., 65
Bandura, A., 8, 25
Barenboim, C., 29
Barkow, J. H., 74
Barresi, J., 52, 53, 54, 56, 59
Bartsch, K., 68
Beating, of children, 13
Behavior-disordered children, 43–45
Behaviors: children's interpretation of others', 69–70; definition of, 19–20; link between moral reasoning and morality of, 43–47; relationship of social cognition to, 69–70
Belief-desire psychology, 21–23
Beliefs: disengaging facts from, 80; false, 25–26, 42, 53, 66, 80; research problems with, 23; versus desires, 21–22

Beliefs, diversity of: children's tolerance of, 10–15; and imagination, 54; studies of, 11–15
Berndt, E. G., 38
Berndt, T. J., 38
Beyond Freedom and Dignity (Skinner, B. F.), 74
Bickhard, M. H., 24
Blame, 26–29, 63–64, 67
Blasi, A., 23, 33
Boyes, M., 24
Braeges, J., 12
Bratman, M. E., 30
Bridgeman, D. L., 79
Buchanan, J. P., 38
Buchsbaum, K., 43

Campbell, J., 22
Capage, L., 46
Capital punishment. *See* Death penalty
Carpendale, J. I., 21, 23, 26, 28, 80
Casas, J. F., 45
Causal conceptions, of the mind, 24
Chandler, M. J., 10, 11, 14, 19, 21, 23, 24, 26, 27, 28, 29, 46, 65, 67, 73, 74, 75, 77, 80
Cheney, R., 67
Children. *See specific age groups*
Churchland, P. M., 20
Classroom behavior, 45–46
Clinchy, B. M., 11
Cobb, R. R., 80
College students, 12, 14
Constructivist process, 8–9
Convention, 11, 78
Copy theory of mind, 24, 33
Corporal punishment, 6, 13
Cosmides, L., 74
Crick, N. R., 45
Cummins, D. D., 68
Cutting, A. L., 45, 46, 65

Dawkins, R., 74
Death penalty, 4, 6
Delay-of-gratification procedure, 55–56, 78–79
Demetriou, H., 45, 46, 65
Deontic reasoning, 68–69

Desires: assumptions about, 74; research problems with, 23; versus beliefs, 21–22
The Development of Social Knowledge (Turiel, E.), 76
Deviant causal chain, 30
Dewey, J., 22
Dockett, S., 46
Dodge, K. A., 43, 44, 69
Domain-specific model, 5, 11, 15, 75–77
Duff, R. A., 23
Duncker, K., 6
Dunn, J., 38, 45, 46, 47, 52, 63, 65
Dunn, L., 58
Dworkin, R. M., 3

Elderly parents, 7
Elfenbein, D., 4
Empathy, 55
Epistemic reasoning, 68–69
Euthanasia, 7

Facts: children's judgment about interplay of, 9–15; disengaging moral beliefs from, 80; distinctions among, 14; interplay with moral beliefs, 5–9; mistaken belief in, 7–8; process of coming to know, 7–8; as rationalizations, 8–9
Fact-value distinction: children's judgment about, 9–15; interplay of moral and factual beliefs in, 5–9; Kohlberg's view of, 3–5, 15
False beliefs, 25–26, 42, 53, 66, 80
Farnill, D., 38
Fincham, F. D., 27
Flavell, E. R., 11, 38
Flavell, J. H., 11, 65
Folk psychology, 65
Ford, S., 6, 13, 47, 64
Forguson, L., 38, 53
Frame, C. L., 43, 44
Frankena, W. K., 3
Frankfurt, H. G., 20
From Is to Ought: How to Commit the Naturalistic Fallacy and Get Away with It (Kohlberg, L.), 3
Frye, D., 38, 52
Furrow, D., 53, 58, 68

Global stage model, 5
Gopnik, A., 20, 21, 22, 23, 29, 38, 53, 54, 58, 64, 75
Green, F. L., 11

Greenspan, S., 29
Gruber, S., 66, 67
Gutkin, D. C., 38

Hacker, P.M.S., 20, 23
Hallett, D., 11, 14, 21, 27, 46
Hare, R. M., 3
Harré, R., 22
Harris, P. L., 21, 53, 54
Hazlitt, W., 52
Hebble, P. W., 38
Heider, F., 1, 23
Helwig, C., 7, 15–16, 78, 79, C.
Henseler, S., 65
Hickling, A., 24
Hildebrandt, C., 4, 6, 15, 78
Hindus, 79
Hobson, R. P., 23
Hofer, B. K., 10
Homer, B. D., 44
Hughes, C., 46–47, 52, 65
Hume, D., 3, 67

Imagination, 54, 55
Imamoglu, E. O., 38
Inhelder, B., 64
Intentions, 29–32, 38–39, 67, 78. *See also* Motivation
Interpretive theory of mind, 24–33
Is-to-ought fallacy: interplay of moral and factual beliefs in, 5–9; Kohlberg's view of, 3–5, 15

Jenkins, J. M., 52
Jewsuwan, R., 45
Jones, C., 19, 21, 73, 74, 75, 77, 80
Joseph, R. M., 29

Kahn, P. H., Jr., 73, 78, 80
Kalish, C., 11, 14
Kant, I., 1, 37
Karniol, R., 38
Keasey, C. B., 38, 39, 43
Keenan, T., 52
Kenny, A., 29
Killen, M., 7, 15–16, 79
Kim, J., 20
Knobe, J., 30
Kohlberg, L., 1, 3, 4, 75
Kostelnik, M., 45
Krettenauer, T., 11, 14
Kuhl, P. K., 75
Kuhn, D., 65, 67

Lalonde, C., 11, 21, 23, 26, 65, 80
Language: epistemic use of, 68; of intentions, 29; in theory-of-mind research, 75
Larkey, C., 38
Lau, A., 40
Laupa, M., 6, 12
Lee, J., 8
Leekam, S., 38, 42, 67
Lemmon, K., 55
Locke, J., 52
Lourenco, O., 80
Luster, T., 45

Macgillivray, S., 51, 78–79
MacIntyre, A. C., 3
Mahapatra, M., 79
Maianau, C., 6, 13, 70
Malle, B. F., 23, 30, 38, 65
Mansfield, A., 11
Marini, A., 44
Martin, R., 52
Mauthner, N., 52
McKeough, A., 44
McNaughton, D., 21, 22
Meltzoff, A., 23, 29, 53, 54, 75
Mentalizing ability, 66
Miller, J. B., 79
Miller, P. H., 38, 65
Mindreading, 66
Mischel, W., 33, 55, 60
Moore, C., 38, 46, 51, 52, 53, 54, 55, 56, 58, 59, 60, 68, 78
Moral beliefs: children's judgment about interplay of, 9–15; children's tolerance of others', 10–15; interplay of facts and, 5–9
Moral concepts: attainment of, by preschoolers, 5; children's agreement about, 6; children's judgment about interplay of, 9–15
Moral judgments: development of, 75; importance of motivation in, 38; interplay of factual and moral beliefs in, 5–9; source of, 4
Moral reasoning, motives-based: and false-belief understanding, 42; link between morality of children's own behavior and, 43–47; overview of, 38; past research on, 38–39; use of motives in, 39–43
Moral reasoning research: focus of, 64, 65, 67–68; future of, 77–81; gap between theory-of-mind research and, 63–70; on motives-based reasoning, 38–39
Moral relativism, 7
Morality, 11, 26–29, 73–75
Moses, L. J., 11, 37–38, 39, 43, 65
Mosher, M., 45
Motivation: and behavior evaluation, 39–43; children's interpretations of, 43–45; and imagination, 55; importance of, in moral reasoning, 38; and interpretive theory of mind, 25; and punishment, 41–42; versus outcomes of actions, 38–39. *See also* Intentions
Mumme, D. L., 11
Murphy, R. R., 43

Nelson, K., 65
Nelson, S. A., 29, 38, 39, 43
Nelson–Le Gall, S. A., 38
Nixon, C. L., 46
Noncurrent goals or interests, 51, 54–55
Nucci, L., 8, 77

Objects of judgment, 5
Olson, D. R., 52, 53, 65

Paul, D., 21
Peabody Picture Vocabulary Test, 31, 58, 59, 60
Peake, P., 60
Peer competence, 45–46
Perner, J., 11, 21, 22, 23, 25, 42, 44, 66, 67
Personal domain, 11, 77
Perspective taking, 64, 65
Philosophy of Mind (Kim, J.), 20
Physical harm: and children's tolerance of others' beliefs, 13; and interpretive theory of mind, 27–29; moral acceptance of, 6–7
Piaget, J., 1, 27, 32, 33, 38, 63–64, 77
Pillow, B. H., 24
Pinker, S., 74
Pintrich, P. R., 10
Plesa, D., 65
Pornography, 6
Povinelli, D. J., 55
Praise, 26–29
Preferences, 11
Premack, D., 64

Preschoolers: altruism in, 55–60; attainment of moral concepts by, 5; and intentionality, 38–39; tolerance of others' beliefs by, 13; use of motives in moral reasoning, 39–43
Price, R., 26
Prosocial behavior, 79
Proximal motives, 39
Prudence: definition of, 51, 52; historical considerations of, 52; and theory of mind, 53–60; versus altruism, 52
Psychological domain, 76–77
Punishment, 41–42, 78
Pure, K., 53, 58, 68
Putnam, H., 3

Rationalization, 8–9
Rawls, J., 3
Reid, T., 22
Repacholi, B. M., 29
Representational change, 53
Resources, distribution of, 6
Right-wrong conception, 68
Roberts, C., 27
Rodriguez, M., 60
Ross, L., 15
Ross, S. D., 33
Ruffman, T., 52
Russell, J., 52

Schlagman, N., 12
School-age children: with behavior disorders, 43–45; and diversity of beliefs, 11, 12–15; and intentionality, 38–39; interplay of factual and moral beliefs in, 5–9; tolerance of others' beliefs by, 11; transition to interpretive theory of mind by, 24–25, 26, 33; use of motives in moral reasoning, 39–43
Schult, C. A., 31
Searle, J. R., 21, 30, 74
Second-order beliefs, 67
Sharing, 56, 57–60
Sharpe, S., 52
Sharpen, J., 52
Shaw, L. A., 6, 12, 13, 14, 70
Ship-witch doodle, 26, 27
Shoda, Y., 60
Shweder, R. A., 79
Skinner, B. F., 19, 74
Slomkowski, C., 52
Smetana, J. G., 5, 11, 12, 76, 79

Smith, K., 12
Social cognition, 65, 69–70
Social competence, 37–38, 45–46
Social group functioning, 52
Socially rejected children, 43–45
Society for Research in Child Development, 1
Sokol, B. W., 2, 10, 11, 14, 19, 21, 23, 24, 27, 46, 67, 73, 74, 75, 77, 80
Somerville, S. C., 38
Spiegel, M., 80
Subpersonal components, 22
Sullivan, K., 44
Symons, D., 60

Tager-Flusberg, H., 29, 44
Taylor, R., 33
Teacher reports, 45–46
Theory of mind: and altruism, 53–60; and computational conceptions of the mind, 73–75; definition of, 66; equal applicability of, 53–54; intentions in, 29–32; interpretive, 24–33; and organization of social behavior, 52–60; overview of, 53; passive conception, 24–25, 33; and prudence, 53–60; and tolerance of others' beliefs, 10–15; variability in, 57; and variance of mental states, 53
Theory-of-mind research: computational language in, 75; focus of, 64, 65, 67–68; future of, 77–81; gap between moral reasoning research and, 63–70; problems with, 22–23
Thompson, C., 56, 59
Thompson, S. K., 38
Tidswell, T., 52
Tisak, M. S., 76
Tolerance, 10–15
Tooby, J., 74
Turiel, E., 4, 5, 6, 7, 9, 11, 15, 16, 76, 78, 79

Unexpected transfer task, 25

Velleman, J. D., 20, 22

Wainryb, C., 3, 4, 6, 7, 8, 9, 10, 12, 13, 14, 15, 16, 47, 64, 67, 70, 79–81
Ward, A., 15
Watson, A. C., 46
Weinstock, M., 67

Wellman, H. M., 11, 20, 22, 23, 38, 65, 68
Wertheimer, M., 6
Western culture, 79–80
White, A., 52
White, P. A., 23
Wilson, A., 46
Wilson, M., 40

Wimmer, H., 21, 25, 42, 44, 64, 66, 67
Woodruff, G., 64

Yates, T., 44
Yuill, N., 39, 43

Zaitchik, D., 44
Zelazo, P. D., 40, 65

Back Issue/Subscription Order Form

Copy or detach and send to:
Jossey-Bass, A Wiley Company, 989 Market Street, San Francisco CA 94103-1741
Call or fax toll-free: Phone 888-378-2537 6:30AM – 3PM PST; Fax 888-481-2665

Back Issues: Please send me the following issues at $29 each
(Important: please include series initials and issue number, such as CD99.)

_____

_____

_____

$ _____   Total for single issues

$ _____   SHIPPING CHARGES: SURFACE   Domestic   Canadian
                                 First Item $5.00 $6.00
                               Each Add'l Item $3.00 $1.50
For next-day and second-day delivery rates, call the number listed above.

Subscriptions: Please __start __renew my subscription to *New Directions for Child and Adolescent Development* for the year 2_____ at the following rate:

     U.S.   __Individual $90   __Institutional $195
     Canada   __Individual $90   __Institutional $235
     All Others   __Individual $114   __Institutional $269
     Online Subscription   __Institutional $195

For more information about online subscriptions visit www.interscience.wiley.com

$ _____   Total single issues and subscriptions (Add appropriate sales tax for your state for single issue orders. No sales tax for U.S. subscriptions. Canadian residents, add GST for subscriptions and single issues.)

__Payment enclosed (U.S. check or money order only)
__VISA __MC __AmEx # _____ Exp. Date _____

Signature _____ Day Phone _____
__ Bill Me (U.S. institutional orders only. Purchase order required.)

Purchase order # _____
                   Federal Tax ID13559302   GST 89102 8052

Name _____

Address _____

_____

Phone _____ E-mail _____

For more information about Jossey-Bass, visit our Web site at www.josseybass.com

OTHER TITLES AVAILABLE IN THE
NEW DIRECTIONS FOR CHILD AND ADOLESCENT DEVELOPMENT SERIES
William Damon, Editor-in-Chief

CD102   Enemies and the Darker Side of Peer Relations, *Ernest V. E. Hodges, Noel A. Card*
CD101   Person-Centered Approaches to Studying Development in Context, *Stephen C. Peck, Robert W. Roeser*
CD100   Exploring Cultural Conceptions of the Transition to Adulthood, *Jeffrey Jensen Arnett, Nancy L. Galambos*
CD99   Examining Adolescent Leisure Time Across Cultures: Developmental Opportunities and Risks, *Suman Verma, Reed Larson*
CD98   Science for Society: Informing Policy and Practice Through Research in Developmental Psychology, *Ann Higgins-D'Alessandro, Katherine R. B. Jankowski*
CD97   Talking Sexuality: Parent-Adolescent Communication, *S. Shirley Feldman, Doreen A. Rosenthal*
CD96   Learning in Culture and Context: Approaching the Complexities of Achievement Motivation in Student Learning, *Janine Bempechat, Julian G. Elliott*
CD95   Social Exchange in Development, *Brett Laursen, William G. Graziano*
CD94   Family Obligation and Assistance During Adolescence: Contextual Variations and Developmental Implications, *Andrew J. Fuligni*
CD93   Supportive Frameworks for Youth Engagement, *Mimi Michaelson, Anne Gregor, Jeanne Nakamura*
CD92   The Role of Family Literacy Environments in Promoting Young Children's Emerging Literacy Skills, *Pia Rebello Britto, Jeanne Brooks-Gunn*
CD91   The Role of Friendship in Psychological Adjustment, *Douglas W. Nangle, Cynthia A. Erdley*
CD90   Symbolic and Social Constraints on the Development of Children's Artistic Style, *Chris J. Boyatzis, Malcolm W. Watson*
CD89   Rights and Wrongs: How Children and Young Adults Evaluate the World, *Marta Laupa*
CD88   Recent Advances in the Measurement of Acceptance and Rejection in the Peer System, *Antonius H. N. Cillessen, William M. Bukowski*
CD87   Variability in the Social Construction of the Child, *Sara Harkness, Catherine Raeff, Charles M. Super*
CD86   Conflict as a Context for Understanding Maternal Beliefs About Child Rearing and Children's Misbehavior, *Paul D. Hastings, Caroline C. Piotrowski*
CD85   Homeless and Working Youth Around the World: Exploring Developmental Issues, *Marcela Raffaelli, Reed W. Larson*
CD84   The Role of Peer Groups in Adolescent Social Identity: Exploring the Importance of Stability and Change, *Jeffrey A. McLellan, Mary Jo V. Pugh*
CD83   Development and Cultural Change: Reciprocal Processes, *Elliot Turiel*
CD82   Temporal Rhythms in Adolescence: Clocks, Calendars, and the Coordination of Daily Life, *Ann C. Crouter, Reed W. Larson*
CD81   Socioemotional Development Across Cultures, *Dinesh Sharma, Kurt W. Fischer*
CD80   Sociometry Then and Now: Building on Six Decades of Measuring Children's Experiences with the Peer Group, *William M. Bukowski, Antonius H. Cillessen*
CD79   The Nature and Functions of Gesture in Children's Communication, *Jana M. Iverson, Susan Goldin-Meadow*
CD78   Romantic Relationships in Adolescence: Developmental Perspectives, *Shmuel Shulman, W. Andrew Collins*

CD77	The Communication of Emotion: Current Research from Diverse Perspectives, *Karen Caplovitz Barrett*
CD76	Culture as a Context for Moral Development, *Herbert D. Saltzstein*
CD75	The Emergence of Core Domains of Thought: Children's Reasoning About Physical, Psychological, and Biological Phenomena, *Henry M. Wellman, Kayoko Inagaki*
CD74	Understanding How Family-Level Dynamics Affect Children's Development: Studies of Two-Parent Families, *James P. McHale, Philip A. Cowan*
CD73	Children's Autonomy, Social Competence, and Interactions with Adults and Other Children: Exploring Connections and Consequences, *Melanie Killen*
CD72	Creativity from Childhood Through Adulthood: The Developmental Issues, *Mark A. Runco*
CD69	Exploring Young Children's Concepts of Self and Other Through Conversation, *Linda L. Sperry, Patricia A. Smiley*
CD67	Cultural Practices as Contexts for Development, *Jacqueline J. Goodnow, Peggy J. Miller, Frank Kessel*
CD65	Childhood Gender Segregation: Causes and Consequences, *Campbell Leaper*
CD46	Economic Stress: Effects on Family Life and Child Development, *Vonnie C. McLoyd, Constance Flanagan*
CD40	Parental Behavior in Diverse Societies, *Robert A. LeVine, Patrice M. Miller, Mary Maxwell West*

**NEW DIRECTIONS FOR
CHILD AND ADOLESCENT DEVELOPMENT
IS NOW AVAILABLE ONLINE AT WILEY INTERSCIENCE**

What is Wiley InterScience?

Wiley InterScience is the dynamic online content service from John Wiley & Sons delivering the full text of over 300 leading scientific, technical, medical, and professional journals, plus major reference works, the acclaimed Current Protocols laboratory manuals, and even the full text of select Wiley print books online.

What are some special features of Wiley InterScience?

Wiley Interscience Alerts is a service that delivers table of contents via e-mail for any journal available on Wiley InterScience as soon as a new issue is published online.

EarlyView is Wiley's exclusive service presenting individual articles online as soon as they are ready, even before the release of the compiled print issue. These articles are complete, peer-reviewed, and citable.

CrossRef is the innovative multi-publisher reference linking system enabling readers to move seamlessly from a reference in a journal article to the cited publication, typically located on a different server and published by a different publisher.

How can I access Wiley InterScience?

Visit http://www.interscience.wiley.com.

Guest Users can browse Wiley InterScience for unrestricted access to journal tables of contents and article abstracts, or use the powerful search engine.
Registered Users are provided with a *Personal Home Page* to store and manage customized alerts, searches, and links to favorite journals and articles. Additionally, Registered Users can view free online sample issues and preview selected material from major reference works.
Licensed Customers are entitled to access full-text journal articles in PDF, with select journals also offering full-text HTML.

How do I become an Authorized User?

Authorized Users are individuals authorized by a paying Customer to have access to the journals in Wiley InterScience. For example, a university that subscribes to Wiley journals is considered to be the Customer.
Faculty, staff and students authorized by the university to have access to those journals in Wiley InterScience are Authorized Users. Users should contact their library for information on which Wiley journals they have access to in Wiley InterScience.

ASK YOUR INSTITUTION ABOUT WILEY INTERSCIENCE TODAY!